PRONOUNCING HANDBOOK

OF

WORDS OFTEN MISPRONOUNCED

AND OF

WORDS AS TO WHICH A CHOICE OF PRONUNCIATION IS ALLOWED

BY

RICHARD SOULE

AND

LOOMIS J. CAMPBELL

BOSTON:
LEE & SHEPARD, PUBLISHERS.
NEW YORK:
LEE, SHEPARD & DILLINGHAM,
49 GREENE STREET.

PREFACE.

It is the purpose of this Handbook to report the current usage of the best speakers with regard to such words as are the most liable to be mispronounced, and also to record such words as may be pronounced in either of two ways without any offence to good taste.

In the latter case, that mode which is supported by the greater weight of authority and is the more generally accepted is put first in order.

In the preparation of the book the latest editions of the Quarto Dictionaries of Webster and Worcester have been examined with care, and also the works of the eminent English orthoëpists, Smart, Cull, and Cooley, who make known the best usage of cultivated Englishmen of the present day. Still further research has been made whenever it seemed desirable.

The compilers have noted and carefully considered the cases in which these authorities differ, and have adopted that mode of pronunciation which seemed to them clearly preferable.

As to the use of this book in schools it may be suggested that each page contains a suitable number of words for a single lesson. Different teachers will doubtless adopt different ways of using the book to suit the wants of their classes.

A good way would be to have the words of the lesson written out on the blackboard, without accents or other marks. The pupils should then pronounce the words as they are pointed out by the teacher.

That the book may be the better adapted for use in schools, some preliminary cautions against common errors are given, and short lists of illustrative words are added, to serve the purpose of drill in pronouncing such words correctly.

BOSTON, MASS., 1873.

INTRODUCTION.

1. Marked Letters.

THE following words will serve to indicate the sounds of the marked letters used in the Vocabulary: —

āle, ēat, īce, ōld, ūse, o͞oze, good, ănd, ĕnd, ĭll, ŏn, ŭp, ärm, fȧre. **ow** is sounded as in **owl,** *th* (italicized) as in **then, th** (unitalicized) as in **thin, g̃** as in **get, ch** as in **chop, er** as in **her.** The vowel **a,** when unaccented, at the end of a word, has a brief sound of **ä** (as in **arm**).

An unmarked vowel (except **a**), forming or ending a syllable, has its long or name sound.

The vowel **a** unmarked, forming or ending an *unaccented* syllable, commonly has a slight sound of **a** as in **arm.** But see 30, page xv.

An unmarked vowel, followed in the same syllable by any consonant except **r**, has its short sound. But **ar** is pronounced as in **arm, er** as in **her, or** as in **nor, ur** as in **fur.**

2. Remarks on Certain Sounds.

It may be well to make the following brief remarks in relation to certain points of pronunciation not familiar to most speakers, or in regard to which there is a difference of opinion among orthoëpists.

a *as in* ask, staff, pass, dance, *&c.*

1. Many cultivated speakers give to the vowel in words of this class the sound of **a** as in **and.** Another large class of speakers give in such words the sound of **a** as in **arm.** Those who prefer the first as the proper quality of the element should avoid the drawl or thin, prolonged sound which is sometimes given to it. Some eminent orthoëpists regard this vowel as of an intermediate quality between **a** as in **and** and **a** as in **arm**; and, as those speakers who hold this opinion would probably avoid the extremes of sound sometimes heard, there may be no practical objection to attempting such a pronunciation.

a *as in* fare, *or* e *as in* there.

2. The most eminent orthoëpists in this country and in England give to the vowel **a** or **e** in words of this class the sound of long **a** deprived of its vanishing element **e** (as heard in *pay*, *say*, &c., in which words the *y* may be considered as representing this vanishing element). This practice is better observed by Englishmen than by Americans. In the United States a somewhat lengthened form of **a** as in **and**, although not sanctioned by the Dictionaries, is more commonly given to words of this class, and is not, perhaps, to be condemned. The sound occurs only before **r**, and should be *closely blended* with the slight sound of **u**, as in **urn**, which is heard before **r** in the pronunciation of such words.

3. The compound long vowel sound, generally indicated by **u**, as in **use**, begins with the consonant **y** and ends with **oo**, — **yoo**.

This is the sound heard in the words *unit* (*yoo'-nit*), *cube* (*kyoob*), *mute* (*myoot*), *educate* (*ed'yoo-kate*), &c. But when the compound vowel **u**, or its equivalent, in a monosyllable or an accented syllable, follows *t*, *d*, *l*, *n*, *s*, *th*, or *j* (commonly), the initial element is slighted so as to become a very brief and indistinct sound of **i** as in **ill**; as in *tune*, *duke*, *lunar*, *nude*, *suit*, *enthusiast*, *jewel*.

In both cases the elements composing the sound of **u** must be drawn together and pronounced **in** the same syllable.

After **r**, **ch**, and **sh** the initial element is omitted and only the final element **oo** (long or short) is heard, as in *rule* (*rōōl*), *true* (*trōō*), *truth* (*trōōth*), *fruit* (*frōōt*), *grew* (*grōō*), *chew* (*chōō*), *sure* (*shōōr*), *sugar* (*shŏŏ′gar*). In some words the same effect is produced by **j**, as *jejune* (*je-jōōn′*).

4. When a short sound of **o** occurs before **ss**, **st**, **th**, or the sound of **f**, as in *cross*, *cost*, *broth*, *soft*, *cough*, and in some cases before **ng**, as in *long*, *strong*, it is the practice of the best speakers to give to the **o** a medium sound between **o** as in **on** and **a** as in **fall**.

5. Many speakers in England give to **e**, **ea**, **i**, and **y**, in a few words (as *herd*, *earth*, *girl*, *myrtle*) whose vowel element is commonly pronounced as **u** in **urn**, a sound very nearly like that of **e** as in **end**; but as this distinction is very generally disregarded in this country, and not consistently preserved in England, the sound has received no distinctive mark in the Vocabulary.

3. Cautions against some Common Errors in Pronunciation.

1. **Do not pronounce** ***ing*** **like** ***in;*** **as** ***eve'nin*** **for** ***eve'ning, writ'in*** **for** ***writ'ing.***

Pronounce the following: Speak'ing, read'ing, talk'ing, walk'ing, stop'ping, smok'ing, suppos'ing, expect'ing, cel'ebrating.

2. **Do not pronounce** ***ow*** **like** ***ur*** **or** ***uh;*** **as** ***hol'lur*** **or** ***hol'luh*** **for** ***hol'low, shad'ur*** **or** ***shad'uh*** **for** ***shad'ow.***

Pronounce the following: Bor'row, to-mor'row, nar'row, yel'low, fel'low, wid'ow, pil'low, mel'lowing, swal'lowing.

3. **Do not pronounce** ***ed*** **like** ***id*** **or** ***ud;*** **as** ***unit'id*** **or** ***unit'ud*** **for** ***unit'ed, provid'id*** **or** ***provid'ud*** **for** ***provid'ed.***

Pronounce the following: Rest'ed, resid'ed, decid'ed, regard'ed, exhib'ited, cel'ebrated, excit'ed, delight'ed, support'ed.

4. **Do not pronounce** ***ess*** **like** ***iss;*** **as** ***good'niss*** **for** ***good'ness, bold'niss*** **for** ***bold'ness.***

Pronounce the following: Hard'ness, bad'ness, harm'less, care'less, clear'ness, ful'ness, seam'stress, host'ess, em'press.

5. **Do not pronounce** ***el*** **like** ***il,*** **nor** ***et*** **like** ***it,*** **nor** ***est*** **like** ***ist;*** **as** ***cru'il*** **for** ***cru'el, bask'it*** **for** ***bask'et, for'ist*** **for** ***for'est.***

Pronounce the following: Fu'el, du'el, bush'el,

yet, get, mark'et, hatch'et, rack'et, rock'et, riv'-ulet, hon'est, bold'est, larg'est, small'est, young'-est, strong'est.

6. **Do not pronounce *ent* like *unt*, nor *ence* like *unce;* as *si'lunt* for *si'lent*, *sen'tunce* for *sen'tence*.**

Pronounce the following: Pru'dent, de'cent, mo'ment, gar'ment, mon'ument, gov'ernment, su-perintend'ent, par'liament (par'lĭ-ment), six'pence, pa'tience, expe'rience, superintend'ence.

7. **Do not insert the sound of short *u* before a final *m;* as *hel'um* for *helm*, *chas'um* for *chasm*.**

Pronounce the following: Spasm, whelm, rhythm, phan'tasm, bap'tism, pa'triotism, elm, film, overwhelm', worm.

8. **Do not give the drawling sound *ăōō* for *ou* (i. e. *äōō*); as *căōō* for *cow*, *hăōōs* for *house*.**

Pronounce the following: How, now, ground, sound, bound, found, town, gown, pound, con-found', around', astound'.

9. **Do not sound *sh* before *r* like *s;* as *srub* for *shrub*, *srink* for *shrink*.**

Pronounce the following: Shred, shrine, shriek, shroud, shriv'el, shrunk'en.

10. **Do not sound *wh* like *w;* as *wen* for *when*, *wat* for *what*.**

Pronounce the following: Where, wheat, wharf,

whale, whine, white, whim'per, whis'per, whip'-ping, whit'tle.

11. Do not omit to give the sound of *r* after a vowel in the same syllable, as in *arm, form,* &c., not *ahm, fawum,* &c.

Pronounce the following: Dark, hark, start, chart, are, tar, remark', course, for, nor, door, floor, lord, hon'or, do'nor, short, support', report', pa'per, or'der, horse, purse, warm, alarm'ing, re-turn'ing, reform'ing.

12. Do not add the sound of *r* to a final vowel or diphthong; as *lawr* for *law, ide'ar* for *ide'a*.

Pronounce the following: saw, draw, paw, claw, pota'to, toma'to, com'ma, Em'ma.

13. Do not shorten the sound of long *o* in certain words by leaving off its vanishing element *o͞o*.

Pronounce the following: Boat, bone, broke, choke, cloak, colt, comb, dolt, hole, home, home'-ly, hope, jolt, load, on'ly, road, rogue, smoke, spoke, spok'en, stone, throat, toad, whole, wrote, yoke, bolster.

14. Do not omit the sound of *d* when preceded by *n*; as *stan* for *stand, frenz* for *friends*.

Pronounce the following: Stands, bands, wīnds, wīnds, depends', defends', demands', blind'ness, grand'mother, grand'father, hand'ful.

15. Do not omit the sound of *d* in the terminal letters *lds;* as *wīlz* for *wilds*, *fēlz* for *fields*.

Pronounce the following: Folds, holds, scolds, builds, scalds, unfolds′, child's.

16. Do not omit the sound of *t* when preceded by *c hard* in the same syllable; as *aks* for *acts*, *exak′ly* for *exact′ly*.

Pronounce the following: Facts, tracts, com′-pacts, inspects′, respects′, inducts′, instructs′, cor-rect′ly, direct′ly, ab′stractly, per′fectly.

17. Do not omit the sound of *t* in the terminal letters *sts;* as *fis's* for *fists*, *pes's* for *pests*.

Pronounce the following: Posts, boasts, coasts, hosts, ghosts, accosts′.

18. Do not improperly suppress the vowel sounds in unaccented syllables; as *ev′ry* for *ev′er-y*, *his′try* for *his′to-ry*.

Pronounce the following: Belief′, crock′ery, fam′ily, fa′vorite, des′perate, des′olate, nom′inative, mis′ery, li′brary, sal′ary, com′pany, com′fortable, perfum′ery, mem′ory, vic′tory, slip′pery, part′i-ciple, sev′eral, bois′terous.

19. Do not suppress the sound of *e* or of *i* before *l* or *n* in those words in which it should be articulated; as *lev′l* for *lev′el*, *civ′l* for *civ′il*, *kitch′n* for *kitch′en*, *Lat′n* for *Lat′in*.

Pronounce the following: Trav′el, nov′el, bar′-

rel, par'cel, hov'el, chap'el, quar'rel, sor'rel, pen'-cil, chick'en, lin'en, sud'den, mit'ten, sat'in.

20. Do not sound *e* or *i* before *n* or *l* in those words in which it is properly silent; as *e'ven* for *ev'n*, *heav'en* for *heav'n*, *ba'sin* for *ba'sn*, *haz'el* for *ha'zl*, *e'vil* for *e'vl*.

Pronounce the following: Ha'ven, sev'en, gold'-en, o'pen, short'en, wood'en, wak'en, wid'en, fro'zen.

21. After *r*, *ch*, or *sh* do not give the sound of long *u* when the simple sound of *oo* (long or short) should be heard; as *rule* for *rool*, *fruit*, for *froot*.

Pronounce the following: True, truth, grew, chew, sure, sug'ar, tru'ly, crew, brute, bru'tal, rude, through, cru'el, ru'by, ru'bicund.

22. Do not substitute the sound *oo* for that of long *u*; as *toon* for *tune*, *doo'ty* for *du'ty*.

Pronounce the following: Tube, duke, mute, nude, mu'sic, Tues'day, du'bious, lute, blue, il-lume', illude', in'stitute.

23. The vowel *a* when unaccented, at the end of a word has the sound of ä (as in *far*) somewhat shortened; as *com'ma* not *com'mĭ* nor *commā*.

Pronounce the following: Dra'ma, da'ta, pi'ca,

so′fa, al′gebra, Chi′na, Amer′ica, dilem′ma, mi′ca, alpac′a, a′rea, neb′ula.

24. **Give to the vowel *a* in the unaccented terminal syllables *al, ant, ance,* its short sound, but do not make it prominent.**

Pronounce the following: Na′tional, par′tial, fi′nal, eter′nal, ig′norant, ty′rant, in′stant, fla′grant, vig′ilance, ig′norance, in′stance, fra′grance.

25. **Do not give to the vowel *a* (as in *far*), when unaccented and made brief, the sound of short *u;* as *ŭbase′* for *abase′, ŭrouse′* for *arouse′*.**

Pronounce the following: Abound′, abate′, above′, about′, abridge′, amuse′, fanat′ic, ag′gravate, traduce′.

26. **Do not give to long *e* when unaccented and slightly abridged, the sound of short *u;* as *ŭvent′* for *event′, soci′ŭty* for *soci′ety*.**

Pronounce the following: Emo′tion, vari′ety, sobri′ety, sati′ety, anxi′ety, impi′ety.

27. **Do not give to long *o*, when unaccented and slightly abridged, the sound of short *u;* as *ŭbey′* for *obey′, prŭpose′* for *propose′*.**

Pronounce the following: Opin′ion, obe′dience, provide′, promote′, provoke′, pota′to, tobac′co, posi′tion, soci′ety, el′oquence, disposi′tion, mel′ody, composi′tion.

28. **Do not sound short *o*, when unaccented, as short *u*; as *ŭbscure'* for *obscure'*, *cŭmmit'tee* for *commit'tee*.**

Pronounce the following: Observe', oppose', command', conceal', condi'tion, contain', content', possess'.

29. **Do not lay too much stress on an unaccented syllable or a syllable having a secondary accent; as *pri'ma'ry* for *pri'mary*, *ex'act'ly* for *exact'ly*.**

Pronounce the following: Gigan'tic, precise'ly, salva'tion, loca'tion, vaca'tion, ter'ritory, sec'ondary, mat'rimony, prom'issory, vac'cinated.

30. **In unaccented syllables do not bring out the quality of the vowel too distinctly.**

In many words, "there would be pedantry in scrupulously avoiding the short and easier sounds which the organs are inclined to adopt." For instance, *cab'bage* in common conversation might be *cab'bij*, *pal'ace*, *pal'ăs*, &c.

1. When *a* at the end of an unaccented syllable is followed in the next syllable by *n* or *r*, it has nearly the sound of short *e*, as in *mis'cel-la-ny*, *cus'tom-a-ry*.

2. In the unaccented final syllable *ate*, of adjectives and nouns, the vowel *a* generally has a sound verging toward short *e*, as in *del′i-cate*, *con-sum′mate* (*adj.*).

PRONOUNCING HANDBOOK.

A.

abdomen, ab-do′men, *not* ab′do-men.

abjectly, ab′ject-lĭ, *not* ab-ject′lĭ. So **ab-jectness.**

ablative, ab′la-tiv, *not* ab′l-tiv.

absolutory, ab-sol′u-to-rĭ, *not* ab-so-lu′to-rĭ.

absolve, ab-zolv′ or ab-solv′. So **ab-solved′.**

abstemious, ab-ste′mĭ-us, *not* ab-stem′ĭ-us.

abstractly, ab′strakt-lĭ or ab-strakt′lĭ.

abstruse, ab-stro͞os′, *not* ab-strūs′.

accent (*verb*), ak-sent′, *not* ak′sent.

access, ak-ses′ or ak′ses.

accessory, ak′ses-so-rĭ or ak-ses′so-rĭ.

acclimate, ak-klī′māt, *not* ak′klĭ-māt.

acclimatize, ak-klī′ma-tīz, *not* ak′klĭ-ma-tīz.

accost,[4] ak-kost′, *not* ak-kawst′.

accoutre, ak-ko͞o′ter, *not* ak-kow′ter.

accrue, ak-kro͞o′, *not* ak-krū′.

acetic, a-set′ik or a-se′tik.

acetify, a-set′ĭ-fī or a-se′tĭ-fī.

acorn, a'korn, *not* a'kurn.
acoustics, a-kows'tiks, *not* a-kōōs'tiks.
across,[4] a-kros', *not* a-krawst'.
adamantean, ad-a-man-te'an, *not* ad-a-man'te-an.
address (*noun and verb*), ad-dres', *not* ad'dres.
adept, a-dept', *not* ad'ept.
adjectival, ad'jek-tiv-al or ad-jek-ti'val.
admirable, ad'mĭ-ra-bl, *not* ad-mi'ra-bl. So **ad'-mi-ra-bly.**
adult, a-dult', *not* ad'ult.
adverse, ad'vers, *not* ad-vers'. So **ad'verse-ly.**
advertise, ad'ver-tīz or ad-ver-tīz'. So **ad-ver-tis'er.**
advertisement, ad-ver'tiz-ment or ad-ver-tīz'-ment.
Æneid, e-nē'id, *not* e'ne-id.
aerated, ā'er-āt-ed, *not* ȧr'āt-ed *nor* ā're-āt-ed.
aerie, e'rĭ or a'rĭ.
aerolite, a'er-o-līt, *not* a-ĕr'o-līt.
aeronaut, a'ĕr-o-nawt, *not* a-ĕr'o-nawt.
afflatus, af-flā'tus, *not* af-flä'tus.
again, a-ḡen', *not* a-gān' *nor* a-ḡin'.
agape, a-gäp' or a-gāp'.
aged, a'jed, *not* ājd, except in compounds, as *full-aged.*
aggrandize, ag'gran-dīz, *not* ag-gran'dīz.
aggrandizement, ag'gran-dīz-ment or ag-gran'-dīz-ment.

agile, aj′ĭl, *not* ạj′īl *nor* ā′jīl.
agriculturist, ag-rĭ-kult′ūr-ist, *not* ag-rĭ-kult′ūr-al-ist.
ague, a′gū, *not* a′gōō.
alabaster,[1] ăl′a-bas-ter, *not* ăl-a-bas′ter.
alarum, a-lär′um or a-lăr′um.
albumen, al-bu′men, *not* al′bu-men.
alcove, ăl′kōv or ăl-kōv′.
Aldebaran, ăl-deb′a-ran, *not* ăl-de-ba′ran.
aldermanic, awl-der-man′ik, *not* ăl-der-man′ik.
Aldine, ăl′dīn or ăl′din, *not* ăl-dēn′.
alexandrine, ăl-eks-an′drin, *not* ăl-eks-an′drīn.
algebra, al′je-bra, *not* al′je-brā.
alien, āl′yen, *not* ā′lĭ-en.
aliment, ăl′ĭ-ment, *not* āl′ĭ-ment.
alkali, al′ka-lī or al′ka-lĭ.
alkalify, al-kal′ĭ-fī or al′ka-lĭ-fī.
alkaline, al′ka-lĭn or al′ka-līn.
allegiance, al-le′jance or al-le′jĭ-ance.
allegorist, al′le-go-rist, *not* al-le-go′rist.
allegro [It.], al-le′gro or al-lā′gro, *not* al′le-gro.
allies (*noun and verb*), al-līz′, *not* al′līz.
allopathist, al-lop′a-thist, *not* al′lo-path-ist.
allopathy, al-lop′a-thĭ, *not* al′lo-path-ĭ.
ally (*noun and verb*), al-lī′, *not* al′lī *nor* al′lĭ.
almond, ä′mund, *not* al′mund.
alms, ämz, *not* älmz *nor* ămz.
alpaca, al-pak′a, *not* al-ä-pak′a.

Alpine, al'pĭn or ăl'pīn, *not* ăl'pēn.
also, awl'so, *not* ŏl'so.
altercate, ăl'ter-kāt, *not* awl'ter-kāt. So **al-ter-ca'tion.**
alternate (*adj.*), ăl-ter'nāt, *not* awl-ter'nāt. So **al-ter'nate-ly, al-ter-na'tion.**
alternate (*verb*), ăl-ter'năt, or ăl'ter-nāt.
always, awl'wāz, *not* awl'wuz, *nor* ŏl'wuz.
amateur, am-a-tur' or am-a-tūr', *not* am'a-tōōr.
ambrosia, am-bro'zhĭ-a or am-bro'zha.
ambrosial, am-bro'zhĭ-al or am-bro'zhal.
ameliorate, a-mēl'yo-rāt, *not* a-mēl'ĭ-o-rāt. So **a-mel-io-ra'tion.**
amenable, a-me'na-bl, *not* a-men'a-bl.
amenity, a-men'ĭ-tĭ, *not* a-me'nĭ-tĭ.
America, A-mĕr'ĭ-ka, *not* A-mĕr'ĭ-kĭ.
amour, a-mōōr', *not* am'ōōr.
ancestral, an'ses-tral or an-ses'tral.
anchovy, an-cho'vĭ, *not* an'cho-vĭ *nor* an-ko'vĭ.
ancient, ān'shent, *not* ăn'shent.
and, and, *not* an.
anemone, a-nem'o-ne, *not* an-e-mo'ne.
angel, ān'jel, *not* ăn'jl.
animadvert, an-ĭ-mad-vert', *not* an-ĭ-mad'vert.
annihilate, an-ni'hĭ-lāt, *not* an-nĭ'lāt.
another, an-uth'er, *not* a-nuth'er.
answer,[1] an'ser, *not* än'ser *nor* an'swer.
antarctic, ant-ark'tik, *not* ant-ar'tik.

antepenult, an-te-pe-nult′, *not* an-te-pe′nult.
antifebrile, an-ti-feb′ril or an-ti-fē′bril.
antipodes, an-tip′o-dēz, *not* an′ti-pōdz.
anxiety, angz-ī′e-tĭ, *not* anks-i′e-tĭ.
anywhere, en′ĭ-hwâr, *not* en′ĭ-hwârz.
aorist, a′o-rist, *not* a-o′rist.
aperture, ap′er-tūr, *not* a-per′tūr.
aphelion, a-fe′lĭ-on, *not* a-fēl′yon.
aphthong,[4] ap′thong or af′thong.
apostle, a-pos′l, *not* a-pos′tl *nor* a-paws′l.
apotheosis, ap-o-the′o-sis, *not* ap-o-the-o′sis.
Appalachian, ap-pa-lā′chĭ-an, *not* ap-pa-la′kĭ-an *nor* ap-pa-lăk′ĭ-an.
apparatus, ap-pa-rā′tus, *not* ap-pa-rä′tus.
apparent, ap-pâr′ent, *not* ap-pā′rent.
applicative, ap′plĭ-ka-tiv, *not* ap-plik′a-tiv.
appreciate, ap-pre′shĭ-āt, *not* ap-pre′shāt.
apprentice, ap-pren′tis, *not* ap-prin′tis.
approbative, ap′pro-ba-tiv, *not* ap-pro-ba′tiv.
apricot, a′prĭ-kot, *not* ap′rĭ-kot.
apron, a′purn or a′prun.
aqueduct, ak′we-dukt, *not* āk′we-dukt.
aquiline, ak′we-lin or ak′we-līn.
Arab, ăr′ab or ā′rab.
Arabic, ăr′a-bik, *not* a-ra′bik.
archangel, ark-ān′jel, *not* arch-ān′jel.
archbishop, arch-bish′op, *not* ark′bish-op.
archetype, ar′ke-tīp, *not* ar′che-tīp.

archipelago, ar-kĭ-pel′a-go, *not* arch-ĭ-pel′a-go.
architect, ar′kĭ-tekt, *not* arch′i-tekt. So **ar-chi-tect′ure**.
archives, ar′kīvz, *not* ar′chīvz.
arctic, ark′tik, *not* ar′tik.
arduous, ar′dū-us, *not* ar′do͞o-us.
are, är, *not* ăur.
area, a′re-a, *not* a-re′a.
arid, ăr′id, *not* är′id *nor* ā′rid.
aristocrat, a-ris′to-krat or ar′is-to-krat.
armada, ar-mā′da, *not* ar-mä′da.
armistice, ar′mis-tis, *not* ar-mis′tis.
aroma, a-ro′ma, *not* ăr′o-ma.
aromatize, a-ro′ma-tīz or ar′o-ma-tīz.
arquebuse, ar′kwe-bŭs, *not* ar′kwe-būs.
arrange, ăr-rānj′, *not* ăr-rănj′.
arrogant, ăr′ro-gant, *not* är′ro-gant.
arrow, ăr′ro, *not* är′ro.
arsenic, ar′sen-ik or ars′nik.
artery, ar′ter-ĭ, *not* ar′trĭ.
Asia, a′shĭ-a, *not* a′zha *nor* a′zhe-a.
Asiatic, a-shĭ-at′ik, *not* a-zhe-at′ik.
aspirant, as-pīr′ant, *not* as′pĭ-rant.
aspirate, as′pĭ-rāt, *not* as-pīr′at.
assets, as′sets, *not* as-sets′.
associate, as-so′shĭ-at, *not* as-so′shāt.
association, as-so-shĭ-a′shun, *not* as-so-se-a′shun.
asked,[1] askt, *not* ast.

asthma, ast′ma or az′ma. So **asth-mat′ic.**
asylum, a-sī′lum, *not* as′ĭ-lum.
asymptote, as′imp-tōt, *not* as-imp′tōt.
ate, āt or et.
athenæum, ath-e-ne′um, *not* a-the′ne-um.
attacked, at-takt′, *not* at-tak′ted.
attorney, at-tur′ne, *not* at-tor′ne.
auction, awk′shun, *not* ork′shun.
audacious, aw-dā′shus, *not* aw-dash′us *nor* ow-da′shus.
audience, au′dĭ-ence, *not* aw′jĭ-ence.
aunt, änt, *not* ănt.
aureola, au-re′o-la, *not* au-re-o′la.
aurora borealis, aw-ro′ra–bo-re-ā′lis, *not* au-ro′-ra–bo-re-ä′lis.
auxiliary, awgz-il′ya-rĭ, *not* awgz-il′ĭ-a-rĭ.
avalanche, av′a-länsh or av-a-länsh′ or av′a-lănsh.
avaunt, a-vawnt′, *not* a-vänt′.
avenue, av′e-nū, *not* av′e-nōō.
awful, aw′fŏŏl, *not* aw′fl *nor* or′fl.
awkward, awk′ward, *not* ork′ard.
awry, a-rī′, *not* aw-rī′.
axiom, ak′sĭ-um or aks′yum.
ay or **aye** (*yes*), äĭ, *not* ā.
aye (*always*), ā, *not* ī.
azote, az′ōt or a′zōt.
azure, a′zhur or azh′ur.

B.

bachelor, bach'el-or, *not* bach'ler *nor* bach'el-dur.
bade, bǎd, *not* bād.
badinage, bad-ĭ-näzh' or bad'ĭ-näzh, *not* bad'in-āj.
balcony, bal'ko-nĭ, *formerly* bal-ko'nĭ.
balderdash, bawl'der-dash, *not* bǎl'der-dash.
ballet [Fr.], bal'lā or bal'let.
balm, bäm, *not* bǎlm *nor* bǎm.
balsam, bawl'sam, *not* bǎl'sam.
balsamic, bǎl-sam'ic, *not* bawl-sam'ic.
banana, ba-nä'na or ba-nā'na.
banian, ban'yan or ban-yan'.
barbarous, bar'ba-rus, *not* bar-ba'rĭ-us.
barrel, bǎr'rel, *not* bǎr'ril *nor* bärl.
barouche, ba-rōōsh', *not* ba-rōōch'.
basalt, ba-sawlt', *not* ba-zawlt'.
basket,[1] bas'ket, *not* bas'kit.
bastile, bas-tēl' or bas'tēl.
bastinado, bas-tĭ-nā'do, *not* bas-tĭ-nä'do.
bath, bäth, *not* bǎth.
baths, bä*thz*, *not* bäths *nor* bǎths.
beauteous, bu'te-us, *not* bu'che-us.
beautiful, bū'tĭ-fŏŏl, *not* be-ū'tĭ-fŏŏl.
because, be-kawz', *not* be-kŏz'.
bedizen, be-dīz'n or be-dĭz'n.
bedstead, bed'sted, *not* bed'stid.
Beelzebub, be-el'ze-bub, *not* bēl'ze-bub.

been, bin, *not* ben.
before, be-fōr′, *not* bŭ-fōr′.
begone,[4] be-gon′, *not* be-gawn′.
behalf, be-häf′, *not* be-hăf′.
behemoth, be′he-moth, *not* be-he′moth.
Belial, bēl′yal or be′lĭ-al.
believe, be-lēv′, *not* blēv.
bellows, bel′lus, *not* bel′lōz.
beloved, (*adj.*) be-luv′ed; (*verb*) be-luvd′.
beneath, be-nēth′, *not* be-nēth′.
benzine, ben′zĭn, *commonly* ben-zēn′.
bequeath, be-kwēth′, *not* be-kwēth′.
bestial, best′yal or best′ĭ-al.
bestiality, best-ye-al′ĭ-tĭ or best-yal′ĭ-tĭ.
bestrew, be-strōō′ or be-strō′.
betroth, be-trŏth′, *not* be-trōth′. So **be-troth′al.**
bevel, bev′el, *not* bev′l.
beyond, be-yond′, *not* be-yund′.
biennial, bī-en′nĭ-al, *not* bĭ-en′yal.
binary, bī′na-rĭ, *not* bin′a-rĭ *nor* bi-na′rĭ.
binomial, bī-no′mĭ-al, *not* bĭ-no′mĭ-al.
biography, bī-og′ra-fĭ, *not* bĭ-og′ra-fĭ.
bipartite, bip′ar-tīt or bī-par′tīt.
bison, bī′sun or biz′un.
bissextile, bis-seks′tĭl or bis-seks′tīl.
bitumen, bī-tu′men, *not* bit′u-men.
bivouac, biv′wak or biv′ōō-ak.
blackguard, blag′ard, *not* blak′gard.

blasphemous, blas′fe-mus, *not* blas-fe′mus.
blasphemy, blas′fe-mĭ, *not* blas-fē′mĭ.
blatant, bla′tant, *not* blăt′ant.
bleat, blēt, *not* blăăt (ă prolonged).
blessed (*adj.*), bles′ed, *not* blest.
blithe, blīth, *not* blīth.
blouse, blowz, *not* blows.
boatswain, bōt′swān or bōs′n.
boisterous, bois′ter-us, *not* bois′trus.
bomb, bum, *not* bom. So **bom′bard, bomb′shell.**
bombast,[1] bum′bast or bum-bast′, *not* bom′bast. So **bom-bas′tic.**
bombazine, bum-ba-zēn′, *not* bom-ba-zēn′.
bonnet, bon′et, *not* bun′et.
booth, bōōth, *not* bōōth.
borealis, bo-re-ā′lis, *not* bo-re-ä′lis.
bosom, bŏŏz′um or bōōz′um, *not* bŏŏz′m.
bounteous, bown′te-us, *not* bown′che-us.
bouquet, bōō-kā′ or bōō′kā, *not* bō-kā′.
bourn, bōrn or bōōrn.
bowline, bō′lĭn, *not* bowl′īn.
bowling, bōl′ing, *not* bowl′ing.
bowsprit, bō′sprit, *not* bow′sprit.
bramin, brä′min, *not* brā′min.
bravado, bra-vā′do, *not* bra-vä′do.
bravo, brä′vo or brā′vo.
breeches, brĭch′ez, *not* brēch′ez. So **breech′ing.**
brethren, breth′ren, *not* breth′er-en.

breviary, brĕv′ya-rĭ or brē′vĭ-a-rĭ.
brew, bro͞o, *not* brū.
brigand, brig′and, *not* brĭ-gănd′.
brigantine, brig′an-tīn, *not* brig′an-tin.
bromide, bro′mĭd, *not* bro′mīd.
bromine, bro′mĭn, *not* bro′mīn.
bronchitis, bron-kī′tis, *not* bron-kē′tis.
bronze, brŏnz or brōnz.
brooch, brōch, *not* bro͞och.
broth, brŏth or brawth.
brothel, brŏ*th*′el, *not* brŏth′el.
brougham, bro͞o′am or bro͞om.
bruit, bro͞ot, *not* bro͞o′it.
brutal, bro͞o′tal, *not* brū′tl.
brute, bro͞ot, *not* brūt.
buddhism, bo͝od′izm or bud′izm.
bulletin, bo͝ol′e-tin or bo͝ol′e-tēn.
bulwark, bo͝ol′wark, *not* bŭl′wark.
buoy, bwoi, *not* boi *nor* bo͞oĭ.
buoyant, bwoi′ant, *not* boi′ant *nor* bo͞oĭ′ant. So **buoy′an-cy.**
bureau, bu′ro or bu-ro′.
Burgundy, bur′gun-dĭ, *not* bur-gun′dĭ.
bushel, bo͝osh′el, *not* bo͝osh′l.
business, biz′nes, *not* biz′ĭ-nes.
bustle, bus′l, *not* bus′tl.
butcher, bo͝och′er, *not* bo͞o′cher.
Byzantine, biz′an-tīn or bĭ-zan′tĭn.

C.

cadi, ka'dĭ, *not* ka'dī.
caisson, kās'son or ka-sōōn'.
calcine, kal-sīn' or kal'sĭn.
caldron, kawl'dron, *not* kăl'dron.
calf, käf, *not* kăăf (ă prolonged).
calisthenics, kal-is-then'iks, *not* kal-is'then-iks.
Calliope, kall-lī'o-pe, *not* kal-lĭ-ō'pe.
calm, käm, *not* kăm.
caloric, ka-lŏr'ik or ka-lō'rik, *not* kăl'o-rik.
calve, käv, *not* kăăv (ă prolonged).
calyx, kā'liks or kăl'iks.
camelopard, ka-mel'o-pard, *not* kam-el-lep'ard.
camphene, kam-fēn' or kam'fēn.
camphor, kam'for, *not* kam'fīr.
can, kan, *not* ken.
Canaanite, ka'năn-īt, *not* ka'nā-ăn-īt.
canaille [Fr.], ka-nāl' or ka-nä'il, *not* ka-nel'.
canine, ka-nīn', *not* ka'nīn.
canorous, ka-no'rus, *not* kan'o-rus.
cantata [It.], kan-tä'ta or kan-tā'ta.
caoutchouc, kōō'chŏŏk, *not* ka'ōō-chŏŏk.
capillary, kap'il-la-rĭ or ka-pil'la-rĭ.
capitoline, kap'ĭ-to-līn, *not* kap-ĭ-to'līn.
capon, ka'pn, *not* ka'pon.
caravan, kăr'a-van or kăr-a-van'.
carbine, kar'bīn, *not* kar'bĭn.

carbonaceous, kar-bo-na'shus, *not* kar-bo-na'-se-us.
caret, ka'ret, *not* kăr'et.
Caribbean, kăr-ib-be'an, *not* ka-rib'be-an.
caricature, kăr'ĭ-ka-tūr, *not* kăr'ĭ-ka-chōōr.
carmine, kar'mīn or kar-mīn'.
carry, kăr'rĭ, *not* kĕr'rĭ.
cartel, car-tel' or car'tel.
Carthaginian, kar-tha-jin'ĭ-an, *not* kar-tha-jēn'ĭ-an.
cartridge, kar'trij, *not* kat'rij.
casement, kāz'ment or kās'ment.
cassimere, kas'si-mēr, *not* kaz'i-mēr.
Cassiopea, kas-sĭ-o-pe'a, *not* kas-sĭ-o'pe-a.
castanet, kas'ta-net or kas-ta-net'.
castle, kas'l, *not* kas'tl.
casual, kazh'u-al, *not* kaz'u-al. So **cas'u-ist.**
casualty, kazh'u-al-tĭ, *not* kazh-u-al'ĭ-tĭ.
catch, kăch, *not* kĕch.
catechumen, kat-e-ku'men, *not* kat-e-chu'men.
Caucasian, kaw-ka'shan, *not* kaw-kash'an.
caudal, kau'dal, *not* kau'dl.
cayenne, kā-en', *not* kī-en' *nor* kī-an'.
celibacy, sel'i-ba-sĭ or se-lib'a-sĭ.
cellar, sel'ler, *not* sul'ler.
cement (*noun*), sem'ent or se-ment'.
cement (*verb*), se-ment', *not* sem'ent.
cemetery, sem'e-tĕr-ĭ, *not* sem'e-trĭ.
centenary, sen'te-na-rĭ, *not* sen-ten'a-rĭ.

centrifugal, sen-trif'u-gal, *not* sen-trĭ-fu'gal.
centripetal, sen-trip'e-tal, *not* sen-trĭ-pe'tal.
cephalic, se-fal'ik, *not* sef'al-ik.
cerate, se'rāt, *not* sĕr'āt.
certain, ser'tin, *not* sert'n.
cervine, ser'vīn, *not* ser'vĭn.
chagrin, sha-grēn' or sha-grĭn'.
chair, châr, *not* chēr.
chalcedony, kal-sed'o-nĭ or kal'se-do-nĭ.
chaldron, chawl'drun or chăl'dron.
chalybeate, ka-lib'e-āt, *not* cha-lib'e-āt
cham, kam, *not* cham.
chamber, chām'ber, *not* chăm'ber.
chamois, sham'ĭ or sha-moi'.
champ, chămp, *not* chomp.
chaos, ka'os, *not* ka'us, *nor* cha'os.
character, kar'ak-ter, *not* ka-rak'ter.
characteristic, kăr-ak-ter-is'tik, *not* krak'ter-is-tik.
chasm, kazm, *not* kaz'um.
chasten, chās'n, *not* chăs'n.
chastisement, chas'tĭz-ment, *not* chas-tīz'ment.
chemise, she-mēz', *not* she-mēs'.
chemistry, kem'is-trĭ or kim'is-trĭ.
chest, chest, *not* chist.
chew, chōō, *not* chū.
chicanery, shē-kān'er-ĭ, *not* shī-kān'er-ĭ.
chicken, chick'en, *not* chick'n *nor* chick'ing.

child, chīld, *not* chīl.
children, chil'dren, *not* chil'durn.
chimera, kī-me'ra, *not* chī-me'ra.
chimerical, kī-mĕr'ik-al, *not* chī-mĕr'ik-al.
chimney, chim'nĭ, *not* chim'lĭ *nor* chim'blĭ.
chimpanzee, chim-pan'ze, *not* shim-pan'ze.
Chinese, chi-nēz', *not* chi-nēs'.
chirography, kī-rog'ra-fĭ, *not* chī-rog'ra-fĭ *nor* kĭr-og'ra-fĭ.
chiropodist, kī-rop'o-dist, *not* chī-rop'o-dist. So **chi-rop'o-dy**.
chisel, chiz'el, *not* chiz'l.
chivalric, shĭ-val'rik or shĭv'al-rik.
chivalrous, shiv'al-rus, *not* shĭ-val'rus.
chivalry, shiv'al-rĭ or chiv'al-rĭ.
chloride, klo'rĭd, *not* klo'rīd.
chlorine, klo'rĭn, *not* klo'rīn.
chocolate, chŏk'o-lāt, *not* chawk'o-lāt.
Christianity, krist-yan'ĭ-tĭ or kris-tĭ-ăn'ĭ-tĭ.
Christmas, kris'mas, *not* krist'mas.
chronological, krŏn-o-loj'ĭk-al or krō-no-loj'ĭk-al.
chyle, kīl, *not* chīl.
cicatrice, sik'a-trĭs, *not* sik'a-trīs.
cinchona, sin-ko'na, *not* sin-cho'na.
circuitous, sur-ku'it-us, *not* sur'kit-us.
citizen, sit'ĭ-zn, *not* sit'ĭ-zen.
civil, siv'il, *not* siv'l.
clandestine, klan-des'tĭn, *not* klan-des'tīn.

clangor, klang'gor, *not* klang'or. So **clang'orous.**

clapboard, klab'bōrd, *not* klab'urd.

cleanly (*adj.*), klĕn'lĭ.

cleanly (*adverb*), klēn'lĭ.

clerk, klerk or klark. The latter is universal in England, the former in the United States.

climacteric, kli-mak-tĕr'ik or kli-mak'ter-ik.

clinch, klinch, *not* klench.

cloth, klŏth or klawth.

cloths, klŏ*th*z or klaw*th*z, *not* klŏths.

clothes, klō*th*z, *colloquially* klōz.

coadjutant, ko-ad'ju-tant, *not* ko-ad-ju'tant.

coadjutor, ko-ad-ju'tor, *not* ko-aj'u-tor.

cobalt, ko'bawlt or ko'bŏlt.

cochineal, kŏch'i-nēl, *not* kōch'i-nēl.

cockatrice, kok'a-trīce, *not* kok'a-trĭs.

cockswain, kok'swān or kok'sn.

co-exist, ko-egz-ist', *not* ko-eks-ist'.

coffee, kof'e, *not* kaw'fe.

coffin, kŏf'in, *not* kawf'in.

cognizance, kog'nĭ-zance or kon'ĭ-zance.

cognizant, kog'nĭ-zant or kon'ĭ-zant.

colchicum, kol'kĭ-kum or kol'chĭ-kum.

coliseum, kol-i-se'um, *not* kol-iz'e-um.

collation, kol-la'shun, *not* co-la'shun.

collusive, kol-lu'siv, *not* kol-lu'ziv.

colon, kō'lon, *not* kō'ln.

colportage, col′pōrt-āj, *not* col-pōrt′āj.
colporter, col′pōrt-er, *not* col-pōrt′er.
column, kol′um, *not* kol′yōōm *nor* kol′yum.
comatose, ko′ma-tōs or kom-a-tōs′.
combat (*noun and verb*), kom′bat or kum′bat.
combatable, kom′ba-ta-bl or kum′ba-ta-bl or kom-bat′a-bl.
combatant, kom′ba-tant or kum′ba-tant, *not* kom-bat′ant.
combative, kom′ba-tiv or kum′ba-tiv, *not* kom-bat′iv. So **com′bat-ive-ness.**
comely, kum′lĭ, *not* kōm′lĭ. So **come′li-ness.**
commensurable, kom-men′shōō-ra-bl, *not* kom-men′zhōō-ra-bl. So **com-men-su-ra-bil′i-ty, com-men′su-rate, com-men-su-ra′tion.**
comment (*verb and noun*), kom′ment, *not* kom-ment′.
commiserate, kom-miz′er-āt, *not* kom-mis′er-āt.
commonwealth, kom′mon-welth or kom-mon-welth′.
communist, kom′mu-nist, *not* kom-mu′nist.
comose, ko-mōs′ or ko′mōs.
comparable, kom′pa-ra-bl, *not* kom-pȧr′a-bl.
compeer, kom-pēr′, *not* kom′pēr.
compensate, kom-pen′sāt or kom′pen-sāt.
compensative, kom-pen′sa-tiv, *not* kom′pen-sa-tiv.
complaisance, kom-pla-zance′ or kom′pla-zance, *not* kom-pla′sance.

complaisant, kom-pla-zant′ or kom′pla-zant, *not* kom-pla′sant.
component, kom-po′nent, *not* kom′po-nent.
composite, kom-poz′ĭt, *not* kom′po-zit.
compost, kom′pōst, *not* kom′pŏst.
compromise, kom′pro-mīz, *not* kom-prom′ĭs.
comrade, kom′răd, *not* kom′rad *nor* kum′rad.
concave, kong′kāv, *not* kon′kāv.
concentrate, kon-sen′trāt or kon′sen-trāt.
conch, kongk, *not* konch.
concise, kon-sīs′, *not* kon-sīz′.
conclusive, kon-clu′siv, *not* kon-klu′ziv.
concourse, kong′kōrs, *not* kon′kōrs.
concrete (*adj. and noun*) kong′krēt or kon′krēt.
condemner, kon-dem′ner, *not* kon-dem′er.
condemning, kon-dem′ning, *not* kon-dem′ing.
condolence, kon-do′lence, *not* kon′do-lence.
conduit, kun′dit or kon′dit.
confessor, kon-fes′ur or kon′fes-ur.
confidant, kon-fĭ-dant′, *not* kon′fĭ-dant.
confine (*noun*), kon′fīn or kon-fīn′.
confiscate, kon-fis′kāt or kon′fis-kāt.
confluent, kon′flu-ent, *not* kon-flu′ent.
confront, kon-frunt′, *not* kon-front′.
congenial, kon-jēn′ĭ-al or kon-jēn′yal. So **con genial′ity.**
congruent, kong′grōō-ent, *not* kon-grōō′ent. So **con′gru-ence.**

conjure (*to practise magic*), kun′jur, *not* kon′jur.
connate, kon-năt′ or kon′năt.
connoisseur, kon-nis-sur′ or kon-nis-sūr′.
conquer, kong′ker, *not* kon′ker *nor* kon′kwer.
conqueror, kong′ker-er, *not* kongk′rer.
conservator, kon′ser-va-tor or kon-ser-va′tor.
considerable, kon-sid′er-a-bl, *not* kon-sid′ra-bl.
consistory, kon′sis-to-rĭ or kon-sis′to-rĭ.
consols, kon-solz′ or kon′solz.
conspiracy, kon-spĭr′a-sĭ, *not* kon-spi′ra-sĭ.
construe, kon′stro͞o, *not* kon-stro͞o′ *nor* kon′ster.
consummate (*verb*), kon-sum′māt or kon′sum-māt.
consummate (*adj.*), kon-sum′māt, *not* kon′sum-māt.
contemner, kon-tem′ner, *not* kon-tem′er. So **con-tem′ning.**
contemplate, kon-tem′plāt or kon′tem-plāt.
contemplator, kon-tem′pla-tor, or kon′tem-pla-tor.
contents, kon-tents′ or kon′tents.
contour, kon-to͞or′, *not* kon′to͞or.
contrary, kon′tra-rĭ, *not* kon′trĭ *nor* kon-tra′rĭ.
contribute, kon-trib′ūt, *not* kon′trĭ-būt *nor* kon-trib′ŭt.
controvert, kon′tro-vert, *not* kon-tro-vert′.
contumacy, kon′tu-ma-sĭ, *not* kon-tu′ma-sĭ.
contumely, kon′tu-me-lĭ, *not* kon-tu′me-lĭ.
convenient, kon-vēn′yent or kon-vēn′ĭ-ent. So **conven′ience.**

conversant, kon'ver-sant, *not* kon-ver'sant.
conversely, kon'vers-lĭ or kon-vers'lĭ.
convex, kon'veks, *not* kon-veks'. So **con'vex-ly**
convivial, kon-viv'ĭ-al or kon-viv'yal.
convoy (*verb*), kon-voy'; (*noun*), kon'voy.
cony, ko'nĭ, *colloquially* kun'ĭ.
cooper, kōōp'er or kŏŏp'er.
copaiba, ko-pa'ba, *not* ko-pe'ba.
coquet (*verb*), ko-ket', *not* ko-kwet'.
coquette (*noun*), ko-ket', *not* ko-kwet'.
coquetry, ko-ket'rĭ, *not* ko'ket-rĭ.
coral, kor'al, *not* ko'ral.
cordial, kord'yal or kor'dĭ-al. So **cordial'ity.**
corollary, kor'ol-la-rĭ, *not* ko-rol'la-rĭ.
coronal, kor'o-nal or ko-ro'nal.
corridor, kor'rĭ-dōr, *not* kor'rĭ-dor.
corse, kors or kōrs.
coruscate, ko-rus'kāt or kor'us-kāt.
corvine, kor'vīn, *not* kor'vĭn.
cost, kŏst or kawst. So **cost'ly.**
costume, kos-tūm' or kos'tūm.
coterie, kō-te-rē', *not* kō'te-rē *nor* kŏt'er-e.
cotyledon, kot-ĭ-le'don, *not* ko-tĭ-le'don.
cotyledonous, kot-ĭ-led'on-us or ko-tĭ-le'don-us.
coupon, kōō'pon, *not* ku'pon.
courier, kōō'rĭ-er, *not* kur'rĭ-er *nor* kōō'rēr.
courteous, kurt'e-us or kōrt'yus.
courtesan, kurt'e-zan, kurt-e-zan' or kōrt'e-zan.

courtesy (*a depression of the body*), kurt'sĭ, *not* kurch'ĭ.
covenant, kuv'e-nant, *not* kov'e-nant.
covetous, kuv'et-us, *not* kuv'e-chus.
cowardice, kow'ar-dĭce, *not* kow'ar-dīce.
cranberry, kran'bĕr-rĭ, *not* kram'brĭ.
craunch, kränch, *not* krawnch.
credence, kre'dence, *not* krĕd'ence.
creek, krēk, *not* krik.
crept, krept, *not* krep.
crinoline, krin'o-lĭn or krin'o-līn.
crocodile, krok'o-dīl, *not* krok'o-dĭl.
crouch, krowch, *not* krōōch.
crude, krōōd, *not* krūd.
cruel, krōō'el, *not* krū'el.
cruise (*to sail to and fro*), krōōz, *not* krōōs.
crupper, krup'er or krŏŏp'er.
cruse, krōōs, *not* krōōz.
cucumber, ku'kum-ber, *not* kow'kum-ber.
cuirass, kwe-răs' or kwe'ras.
culinary, ku'lĭ-na-rĭ, *not* kul'ĭ-na-rĭ.
cupola, ku'po-la, *not* ku'pa-lo.
curator, ku-ra'tor, *not* ku'ra-tor.
current, kur'rent, *not* kurnt.
cursed (*adj.*), kur'sed, *not* kurst.
curtain, kur'tin, *not* kurt'n.
cushion, kŏŏsh'un, *not* kwish'un.
cyclopean, si-klo-pe'an, *not* si-klo'pe-an.
cynosure, si'no-shōōr or sin'o-shōōr.

D.

daguerreotype, da-ḡĕr′o-tīp, *not* da-ḡĕr′e-o-tīp.
dahlia, däl′ya or dāl′ya.
damning, dam′ning, *not* dam′ing.
dandelion, dan′de-li-on or dan-de-li′on, *not* dan′-de-līn.
Danish, dān′ish, *not* dan′ish.
data, dā′ta, *not* dä′ta.
daub, dawb, *not* dob.
daunt, dänt, *not* dawnt.
deaf, dĕf, *not* dēf. So **deaf′en.**
decade, dek′ād, *not* dek-ād′.
decadence, de-kā′dence, *not* dek′a-dence.
decantation, de-kan-ta′shun or dek-an-ta′shun.
declarative, de-klăr′a-tĭv, *not* de-klár′a-tĭv.
decorous, de-ko′rus or dek′o-rus.
decrepit, de-krep′it, *not* de-krep′id.
defalcate, de-făl′kāt, *not* def′ăl-kāt *nor* de-fawl′-kāt.
defalcation, de-făl-ka′shun or def-al-ka′shun.
deficit, def′ĭ-sit, *not* de-fis′it.
defile (*noun*), de-fīl′ or de′fīl.
delivery, de-liv′er-ĭ, *not* de-liv′rĭ.
demise, de-mīz′, *not* de-mīs′.
demonstrate, de-mon′strāt or dem′on-strāt.
demonstration, dem-on-stra′shun, *not* de-mon-stra′shun.

demonstrative, de-mon′stra-tiv, *not* dem′on-stra-tiv.

demonstrator, dem′on-stra-tur, *not* de-mon′stra-tur.

denationalize, de-nash′un-al-īz, *not* de-na′shun-al-īz.

denudation, den-u-da′shun or de-nu-da′shun.

denunciate, de-nun′shĭ-āt, *not* de-nun′shāt.

depends, de-pends′, *not* de-penz′.

deposition, dep-o-zish′un or de-po-sizh′un.

depot, dē-po′ or dā-po′, *but commonly* dē′po.

depreciate, de-pre′shĭ-āt, *not* de-pre′shāt.

depths, depths, *not* deps *nor* debths.

deputy, dep′u-tĭ, *not* deb′u-tĭ.

derelict, dĕr′e-likt, *not* dĕr-e-likt′.

dereliction, dĕr-e-lik′shun, *not* dĕr-e-lek′shun.

derisive, de-ri′sĭv, *not* de-ri′zĭv.

desiccate, de-sik′kāt or des′ik-kāt.

design (*noun and verb*), de-sīn′ or de-zīn′.

designate, des′ig-nāt, *not* dez′ig-nāt *nor* de-sig′-nāt.

desist, de-sist′, *not* de-zist′.

desolate, des′o-lāt, *not* dez′o-lāt. So **des-o-la′-tion.**

desperado, des-pe-rā′do, *not* des-pe-rä′do.

despicable, des′pĭ-ka-bl, *not* des-pik′a-bl.

destine, des′tĭn, *not* des′tīn.

desultory, des′ul-to-rĭ, *not* de-zult′o-rĭ.

detail (*noun*), de'tāl or de-tāl'; (*verb*), de-tāl'.
detestation, det-es-ta'shun or de-tes-ta'shun.
devastate, dev as-tāt or de-văs'tāt.
devil, dev'l, *not* dev'il.
dew, dū, *not* dōō.
diæresis, dī-ĕr'e-sis, *not* di-e-re'sis *nor* di-e're-sis.
dialogue, dī'a-lŏg, *not* dī'a-lawg.
diamond, dī'a-mund or dī'mund.
diatribe, di'a-trīb, *not* di-at'ri-be.
didactic, dĭ-dak'tik, *not* dī-dak'tik.
different, dif'fer-ent, *not* dif'rent.
differentiate, dif-fer-en'shĭ-āt, *not* dif-fer-en'shāt.
diffuse (*adj.*), dif-fūs', *not* dif-fūz'.
diffusive, dif-fu'sĭv, *not* dif-fu'zĭv.
digression, dĭ-gresh'un, *not* dī-gresh'un.
dilapidate, dĭ-lap'ĭ-dāt, *not* dī-lap'ĭ-dāt.
dilate, dĭ-lāt' or dī-lāt'.
dilemma, dĭ-lem'ma or dī-lem'ma.
dimension, dĭ-men'shun, *not* dī-men'shun.
diocesan, dī-os'e-san or dī-o-sē'san.
diocese, dī'o-sēs or dī'o-sēs.
diorama, di-o-rā'ma or di-o-rä'ma.
diphtheria, dif-the'rĭ-a, *not* dip-the'rĭ-a.
diphthong, dip'thong or dif'thong.
diploma, dĭ-plo'ma, *not* dī-plo'ma.
diplomacy, dĭ-plo'ma-sĭ, *not* dip'lo-ma-sĭ.
diplomatic, dip-lo-mat'ik, *not* dī-plo-mat'ik.
diplomatist, dĭ-plo'ma-tist, *not* dī-plo'ma-tist.

direct, dĭ-rekt′, *not* dī-rekt′ *nor* drekt.
disable, dis-a′bl or diz-a′bl.
disarm, diz-arm′, *not* dis-arm′.
disaster, diz-as′ter, *not* dis-as′ter.
disband, dis-band′ or diz-band′.
disburden, dis-bur′dn or diz-bur′dn.
disburse, dis-burse′ or diz-burse′.
discern, diz-zern′, *not* dis-sern′. So **dis-cern′-ment.**
discourteous, dis-kurt′e-us, *not* dis-kōrt′e-us.
discoverer, dis-kuv′er-er, *not* dis-kuv′rer.
discovery, dis-kuv′er-ĭ, *not* dis-kuv′rĭ.
discrepance, dis′kre-pance or dis-krep′ance. So **discrepancy, discrepant.**
disdain, diz-dān′, *not* dis-dān′.
disease, diz-ēz′, *not* dis-ēz′.
disfranchise, dis-fran′chĭz, *not* dis-fran′chīz.
disgorge, dis-gorj′ or diz-gorj′.
disgrace, dis-grāce′ or diz-grāce′.
disguise, dis-ḡīz′ or diz-ḡīz′.
disgust, dis-gust′ or diz-gust′.
dishabille, dis-ha-bĭl′, *not* dis-ha-bēl′.
dishevelled, dĭ-shev′ld, *not* dis-hev′ld.
dishonest, diz-on′est, *not* dis-on′est. So **dis-hon′or, dis-hon′or-a-ble, dis-hon′es-ty.**
disinterested, dis-in′ter-est-ed or diz-in′ter-est-ed, *not* dis-in-ter-est′ed.
disjoin, dis-join′ or diz-join′.

disjoint, dis-joint′ or diz-joint′.
disjunctive, dis-junc′tiv or diz-junc′tiv.
dislike, dis-līk′ or diz-līk′.
dislodge, dis-loj′ or diz-loj′.
disloyal, dis-loy′al or diz-loy′al.
dismantle, dis-man′tl or diz-man′tl.
dismast,[1] dis-mast′ or diz-mast′.
dismay, dis-mā′ or diz-mā′.
dismember, dis-mem′ber or diz-mem′ber.
dismiss, dis-mis′ or diz-mis′.
dismount, dis-mownt′ or diz-mownt′.
disoblige, dis-o-blīj′, *not* dis-o-blēj′.
disorder, dis-or′der or diz-or′der.
disorganize, dis-or′gan-īz or diz-or′gan-īz.
disown, dis-ōn′ or diz-ōn′.
dispossess, dis-poz-zes′, *not* dis-pos-ses′.
disputable, dis′pu-ta-bl, *not* dis-pu′ta-bl.
disputant, dis′pu-tant, *not* dis-pu′tant.
disrobe, dis-rōb′ or diz-rōb′.
disruption, dis-rup′shun or diz-rup′shun.
dissemble, dis-sem′bl, *not* diz-zem′bl.
dissociate, dis-so′shĭ-āt, *not* dis-so′shāt.
dissolve, diz-zolv′, *not* dis-solv′.
dissyllable, dis-sil′la-bl or dis′sil-la-bl.
distich, dis′tik, *not* dis′tich.
district, dis′trikt, *not* de′strikt.
divan, dĭ-van′, *not* dī′van.
divaricate, dī-văr′ĭ-kāt, *not* dĭ-văr′ĭ-kāt.

diverge, dĭ-verj′, *not* dī-verj′.
diverse, di′verse, *not* di-verse′. So **di′verse-ly.**
divert, dĭ-vert′, *not* dī-vert′.
divest, dĭ-vest′, *not* dī-vest′.
divulge, dĭ-vulj′, *not* dī-vulj′.
do, do͞o, *not* dĭo͞o.
docile, dos′ĭl, *not* do′sīl.
does, duz, *not* do͞oz.
dog, dŏg, *not* dawg.
dolorous, dŏl′o-rus, *not* dō′lo-rus.
domain, do-mān′, *not* do′mān.
domicile, dom′ĭ-sĭl, *not* dom′ĭ-sīl.
dominie, dŏm′ĭ-nĭ, *not* dō′mĭ-nĭ.
donative, don′a-tĭv, *not* do′na-tĭv.
donkey, dong′kĭ, *not* dung′kĭ.
Doric, dŏr′ik, *not* dō′rik.
dost, dust, *not* dōst.
doth, duth, *not* dōth.
drama, drā′ma or drăm′a.
dramatist, dram′a-tist, *not* drā′ma-tist.
draught,[1] draft, *not* drawt.
drawers, draw′erz, *not* draw′uz *nor* drawz.
drollery, drōl′er-ĭ, *not* drŏl′er-ĭ.
dromedary, drum′e-da-rĭ, *not* drom′e-da-rĭ.
dross,[4] drŏs, *not* draws.
drown, drown, *not* drownd.
drowned, drownd, *not* drown′ded.
Druid, dro͞o′id, *not* drū′id.

ducat, dŭk'at, *not* dū'kat.
ductile, duk'tĭl, *not* duk'tīl.
duet, dū-et', *not* do͞o-et'.
duke, dūk, *not* do͞ok.
duress, du'res or du-res'.
duty, dū'tĭ, *not* do͞o'tĭ.
dwarfs (*n. pl.*), dwawrfs, *not* dwawrvz.
dynasty, dī'nas-tĭ or dĭn'as-tĭ.
dysentery, dis'en-tĕr-ĭ, *not* diz'en-tĕr-ĭ.

E.

early, er'lĭ, *not* ȧr'lĭ.
eastward, east'ward, *not* east'ard.
éclat, ā-klä' or e-klä', *not* e-klaw'.
economical, e-ko-nom'ĭ-kal or ek-o-nom'ĭ-kal.
educate, ed'ū-kāt, *not* ed'ĭ-kāt. So **ed-u-ca'tion.**
e'er, ȧr, *not* ēr.
effort, ef'furt or ef'fōrt.
effrontery, ef-frunt'er-ĭ, *not* ef-frŏnt'er-ĭ.
egg, ĕg, *not* āg.
egotism, e'go-tizm or eg'o-tizm. So **egotist.**
egregious, e-gre'jus or e-gre'jĭ-us.
either, ē'*th*er or ī'*th*er.
eleemosynary, el-e-moz'ĭ-na-rĭ, *not* el-e-mos'ĭ-na-rĭ.
elegiac, e-le'jĭ-ak or el-e-jī'ak.
elephantine, el-e-fan'tĭn, *not* el-e-fan'tīn.

eleven, e-lev′n, *not* levn.
Elizabethan, e-liz′a-beth-an or e-liz-a-beth′an.
elm, elm, *not* el′um.
elusive, e-lu′sĭv, *not* e-lu′zĭv.
Elysium, e-lizh′ĭ-um, *not* e-liz′ĭ-um.
emaciate, e-ma′shĭ-āt, *not* e-ma′shāt.
emendation, em-en-da′shun, *not* ē-men-da′shun.
emolliate, e-mol′lĭ-āt or e-mol′yāt.
emollient, e-mol′yent, *not* e-mol′lĭ-ent.
empiric (*noun*), em-pĭr′ik or em′pĭr-ik.
empyrean, em-pĭ-re′an or em-pĭr′e-an.
encore, ŏng-kōr′, *not* ŏng′kōr.
endive, en′div, *not* en′dīv.
enervate, e-ner′vāt, *not* en′er-vāt.
enfranchise, en-fran′chĭz, *not* en-fran′chīz.
engine, en′jĭn, *not* en′jīn.
enginery, en′jĭn-rĭ, *not* en′jīn-rĭ.
engross, en-grōs′, *not* en-grŏs′ *nor* en-graws′.
ennui, än-we′ or ŏng-we′, *not* ŏng′we.
enunciate, e-nun′shĭ-āt, *not* e-nun′shāt. So **e-nun-ci-a′tion.**
envelope (*noun*), en′ve-lōp or äng′ve-lōp.
environs, en-vi′runz or en′vĭ-runz.
ephemeral, e-fem′er-al, *not* ef-fem′er-al.
epicurean, ep-ĭ-ku-re′an, *not* ep-ĭ-ku′re-an.
epistle, e-pis′l, *not* e-pis′tl.
epitaph, ep′ĭ-tăf, *not* ep′ĭ-täf.
epoch, ep′ok or e′pok.

equable, e'kwa-bl or ek'wa-bl.
equanimity, e-kwa-nim'ĭ-tĭ, *not* ek-kwa-nim'ĭ-tĭ.
equation, e-kwa'shun, *not* e-kwa'zhun.
equatorial, e-kwa-to'rĭ-al, *not* ek-wa-to'rĭ-al.
equerry, ek'wĕr-rĭ or e-kwĕr'rĭ.
equinox, e'kwĭ-noks, *not* ek'wĭ-noks. So **e-qui-noc'tial.**
equipage, ek'wĭ-pej, *not* e-kwip'ej.
equipoise, e'kwĭ-poiz, *not* ek'wĭ-poiz.
ere, âr, *not* ēr.
ermine, er'mĭn, *not* er'mīn.
err, er, *not* ĕr.
errand, ĕr'rand, *not* ăr'ant *nor* er'rand.
erratum, ĕr-rā'tum, *not* ĕr-rä'tum. So **er-ra'ta.**
erring, ĕr'ring or er'ring.
erudite, ĕr'ōō-dīt, *not* ĕr'u-dīt.
erysipelas, ĕr-ĭ-sip'e-las, *not* ĭr-ĭ-sip'e-las.
espionage, es'pe-o-nāj or es'pe-o-näzh.
essayist, es'sa-ist or es-sa'ist.
etiquette, et'ĭ-ket, *not* et'ĭ-kwet.
European, ū-ro-pe'an, *not* ū-ro'pe-an.
euthanasy, ū-than'a-sĭ or ū'than-a-sĭ.
evangelical, e-van-jel'ĭ-kal or ev-an-jel'ĭ-kal.
evasive, e-va'siv, *not* e-va'ziv.
every, ev'er-ĭ, *not* ev'rĭ.
evil, e'vl, *not* e'vil.
exacerbate, egz-as'er-bāt, *not* eks-a-ser'bāt.
exact, egz-akt', *not* eks-akt'.

exaggerate, egz-aj′er-āt, *not* eks-aj′er-āt.
exalt, egz-awlt′, *not* eks-awlt′.
examine, egz-am′ĭn, *not* eks-am′ĭn.
example,[1] egz-am′pl, *not* eks-am′pl.
exasperate, egz-as′per-āt, *not* eks-as′per-āt.
excellent, eks′sel-lent, *not* eks′lent.
excise, eks-sīz′, *not* eks′sīz.
exciseman, eks-sīz′man, *not* eks′sīs-man.
exclusive, eks-clu′sĭv, *not* eks-clu′zĭv.
excretive, eks-kre′tĭv or eks′kre-tĭv.
excretory, eks-kre′to-rĭ or eks′kre-to-rĭ.
excruciate, eks-kroo′shĭ-āt, *not* eks-kroo′shāt.
excursion, eks-kur′shun, *not* eks-kur′zhun.
executive, egz-ek′u-tiv, *not* eks-ek′u-tiv.
executor, egz-ek′u-tor, *not* eks-ek′u-tor. So **ex-ec′u-trix.**
exemplar, egz-em′plar, *not* eks-em′plar.
exemplary, egz′em-pla-rĭ, *not* egz-em′pla-rĭ.
exemplify, egz-em′plĭ-fī, *not* eks-em′plĭ-fī.
exempt, egz-emt′, *not* eks-emt′.
exert, egz-ert′, *not* eks-ert′.
exhale,* egz-hāl′ *commonly* eks-hāl′.
exhaust,* egz-hawst′, *commonly* egz-awst′. So **ex-haust′ion; ex-haust′ive.**
exhibit,* egz-hib′it, *commonly* egz-ib′it. So **ex-hib′i-to-ry.**
exhibition, eks-hĭ-bish′un, *not* egz-ĭ-bish′un.

* See note, page 32.

exhilarate,* egz-hil'a-rāt, *commonly* egz-il'a-rāt.

exhort,* egz-hort', *commonly* egz-ort'. So **exhort'er.**

exhortation, eks-hor-tā'shun, *not* egz-or-ta'shun.

exhume,* egz-hūm', *commonly* eks-hūm'.

exile (*noun*), eks'īl; **exile** (*verb*), eks'īl or egz-īl'.

exist, egz-ist', *not* eks-ist'.

exonerate, egz-on'er-āt, *not* eks-on'er-āt.

exorbitant, egz-or'bĭ-tant, *not* eks-or'bĭ-tant.

exorcise, eks'or-sīz, *not* eks-or'sīz.

exordium, egz-or'dĭ-um, *not* eks-or'dĭ-um.

exoteric, eks-o-tĕr'ik, *not* eks-ot'er-ik.

expatiate, eks-pā'shĭ-āt, *not* eks-pā'shāt.

expert (*noun*), eks'pert or eks-pert'; (*adj.*), eks-pert'.

expiration, eks-pĭ-ra'shun, *not* eks-pī-ra'shun.

expletive, eks'ple-tĭv, *not* eks-ple'tĭv.

explicable, eks'plĭ-ka-bl, *not* ex-plik'a-bl.

exploit, eks-ploit', *not* eks'ploit.

explosive, eks-plo'sĭv, *not* eks-plo'zĭv.

* According to a rule given by the Dictionaries, "*x* has the sound of *gz* when it ends an unaccented syllable and the next syllable is accented and begins with a vowel *or the letter h*." But when this syllable begins with the letter *h*, it is almost the universal custom, in opposition to the Dictionaries, either to drop the sound of *h*, giving *x* the sound of *gz*, or, if the sound of *h* be retained, to give to *x* the sound of *ks*; thus *exhaust* is commonly pronounced *egz-awst'*, and *exhale*, *eks-hāl'*.

exponent, eks-po′nent, *not* eks′po-nent.
expurgate, eks-pur′gāt or eks′pur-gāt.
expurgator, eks-pur′ga-tor or eks′pur-ga-tor.
exquisite, eks′kwĭ-zit, *not* eks-kwiz′it.
extant, eks-tant′, *not* eks′tant.
extempore, eks-tem′po-re, *not* eks-tem′pōr.
extirpate, eks-ter′pāt or eks′ter-pāt. So **extir′-pator.**
extol, eks-tŏl′, *not* eks-tōl′.
extra, eks′trä, *not* eks′trĭ.
extraordinary, eks-tror′dĭ-na-rĭ or eks-tra-or′dĭ-na-rĭ.
extrude, eks-trōōd′, *not* eks-trūd′.
exuberant, egz-yōō′ber-ant, *not* eks-yōō′ber-ant. So **ex-u′ber-ance.**
exude, eks-ūd′, *not* egz-ūd′.
exult, egz-ult′, *not* eks-ult′.
eyry, ȧr′ĭ, *not* ī′rĭ.

F.

fabric, făb′rik, *not* fā′brik.
façade, fa-säd′ or fa-sād′.
facile, fas′ĭl, *not* fas′īl.
fac-simile, fak-sim′i-le, *not* fak-sim′īl.
factory, fak′to-rĭ, *not* fak′trĭ.
falchion, fawl′chun or fawl′shun, *not* făl′chun.
falcon, faw′kn, *not* făl′kn. So **fal′con-er.**

familiarity, fa-mil-yĭ-ăr'i-tĭ or fa-mil-yăr'i-tĭ.
far, far, *not* fur.
farina, fa-rī'na or fa-rē'na.
faro, får'o, *not* făr'o *nor* fa'ro.
farrago, făr-rā'go, *not* făr-rä'go.
faucet, faw'set, *not* fas'et.
favorite, fa'vor-ĭt, *not* fa'vor-īt.
fealty, fe'al-tĭ, *not* fēl'tĭ.
febrile, fe'bril or feb'ril.
February, feb'rōō-a-rĭ, *not* feb'ū-a-rĭ *nor* feb'ĭ-wĕr-rĭ.
fecund, fek'und, *not* fe'kund.
fecundate, fek'un-dāt or fe-kun'dāt.
feme-covert, fem-kuv'ert, *not* fēm-kōō-vert'.
feme-sole, fem-sōl' or fam-sōl', *not* fēm-sōl'.
feminine, fem'ĭ-nĭn, *not* fem'ĭ-nīn.
feoff, fĕf, *not* fe'of *nor* fēf.
ferrule (*a ring*), fĕr'ril or fĕr'rōōl.
fertile, fer'tĭl, *not* fer'tīl.
ferule (*a rule*), fĕr'il or fĕr'ōōl.
fetid, fet'id, *not* fe'tid.
fidelity, fĭ-del'ĭ-tĭ, *not* fī-del'ĭ-tĭ.
fiduciary, fĭ-du'shĭ-a-rĭ, *not* fĭ-du'sha-rĭ.
fierce, fērce, *not* furce.
figure, fig'yur, *not* fig'ur. So **fig'ured.**
film, film, *not* fil'um.
finale, fe-nä'le, *not* fi'nāl.
finance, fĭ-nance', *not* fī'nance. So **fi-nan'cial.**

financier, fin-an-sēr′, *not* fī-nan-sēr′.
finesse, fe-nes′, *not* fī-nes′.
flaccid, flak′sid, *not* flas′id.
flageolet, flaj-o-let′, *not* flaj-e-o-let′.
flaunt, flänt, *not* flawnt.
flew, flū, *not* flōō.
Florentine, flor′en-tīn or flor′en-tĭn, *not* flor′-en-tēn.
florid, flŏr′id, *not* flo′rid.
florin, flŏr′in, *not* flo′rin.
florist, flo′rist, *not* flŏr′ist.
fœticide, fĕt′i-sīd, *not* fēt′i-sīd.
folio, fōl′ĭ-o or fōl′yo.
for, for, *not* fur.
forbade, for-băd′, *not* for-bād′.
forecastle,[1] fōr′kas-l, *not* fōk′a-sl.
forefather, fōr′fä-*th*er or fōr-fä′*th*er.
forehead, fŏr′ed or fōr′hed.
forest, for′est, *not* for′ist.
forge, fōrj, *not* fawrj.
forgery, fōrj′er-ĭ, *not* for′jer-ĭ *nor* fawj′rĭ.
forget, for-get′, *not* for-git′.
formidable, for′mĭ-da-bl, *not* for-mid′a-bl.
forray, fŏr′rā or fŏr-rā′.
fortnight, fort′nīt or fort′nĭt.
fortress, for′tres, *not* fōrt′res.
forty, for′tĭ, *not* faw′tĭ.
forward, for′ward, *not* for′urd.

fountain, fown′tin, *not* fownt′n.
fracas, fra′kus, *not* fra-cä′. In England the latter is preferred.
fragile, fraj′ĭl, *not* fraj′īl.
fragmentary, frag′ment-a-rĭ, *not* frag-ment′a-rĭ.
franchise, fran′chĭz, *not* fran′chīz.
frankincense, frank′in-sense or frank-in′sense.
fraternize, fra-ter′nīz, *not* fra′ter-nīz.
fratricide, frat′rĭ-sīd, *not* fra′trĭ-sīd.
friends, frendz, *not* frenz.
friendship, frend′ship, *not* fren′ship.
frontier, frŏn′tēr or frun′tēr.
frontispiece, frŏnt′is-pēs, *not* frunt′is-pēs.
frost,[4] frŏst or frawst.
froth,[4] frŏth or frawth.
frugal, froo′gal, *not* frū′gl.
fruit, froot, *not* frūt.
fuchsia, fū′shĭ-a or fook′sĭ-a.
fugue, fūg, *not* fūj.
fulcrum, fŭl′crum, *not* fool′crum.
fulsome, fŭl′sum, *not* fool′sum.
furniture, fur′nit-yoor, *colloquially,* fur′nĭ-choor.
fusil (*adj.*), fu′zil, *not* fu′sil.
futile, fu′tĭl, *not* fu′tīl.

G.

gainsay, gān-sā′ or gān′sā.
gallant (*attentive to ladies*), gal-lănt′ or gallänt′.
gallows, gal′lus, *not* gal′lōz.
galoche, ga-lŏsh′ or ga-lōsh′.
gamboge, gam-bōōj′ or gam-bōj′.
gangrene, gang′grēn, *not* gan′grēn.
gape, gäp or gāp, *not* găp. So **gap′ing.**
garden, gar′dn, *not* gar′den.
garrulous, găr′rōō-lus, *not* găr′yōō-lus.
gas, găs, *not* gäs *nor* găz.
gaseous, găz′e-us, *not* găs′e-us.
gasometer, gaz-om′e-ter, *not* gas-om′eter.
gather, ga*th*′er, *not* ḡe*th*′er.
gaunt, gänt, *not* gawnt. So **gaunt′let.**
genealogy, jĕn-e-al′o-jĭ or jē-ne-al′o-jĭ. So **genealog′ical, geneal′ogist.**
generally, jen′er-al-lĭ, *not* jen′rul-lĭ.
genial, jēn′ĭ-al, *not* jēn′yal.
genius (*inborn faculty*), jēn′yus or je′nĭ-us.
genius (*a spirit*), jē′nĭ-us, *not* jēn′yus.
Gentile, jen′tīl, *not* jen′tĭl.
gentlemen, jen′tl-men, *not* jen′tl-mun.
genuine, jen′ū-ĭn, *not* jen′ū-īn.
geography, je-og′ra-fĭ, *not* jog′ra-fĭ.
geometry, je-om′e-trĭ, *not* jom′e-trĭ.
gerund, jĕr′und, *not* je′rund.

get, ḡet, *not* ḡit.
gherkin, gur'kin, *not* jur'kin.
ghoul, gōōl, *not* gowl.
giaour, jowr, *not* jōōr.
gibberish, ḡib'er-ish, *not* jib'er-ish. So **gib'ber**.
gibbet, jib'et, *not* ḡib'et.
gibbous, ḡib'us, *not* jib'us.
gigantean, ji-gan-te'an, *not* ji-gan'te-an.
giraffe, jĭ-raf' or zhe-raf', *not* jī-raf'.
glacial, gla'shĭ-al or gla'shal.
glacier, glas'ĭ-er, *not* gla'sēr.
gladiator, glad'ĭ-a-tur, *not* glā'dĭ-a-tur.
glisten, glis'n, *not* glis'tn.
God, gŏd, *not* gawd.
golden, gōld'n, *not* gōld'en.
gondola, gon'do-la, *not* gon-do'la.
gone, gŏn or gawn.
gooseberry, gōōz'bĕr-rĭ, *not* gōōs'bĕr-rĭ.
Gordian, gor'dĭ-an, *not* gord'yan.
gorgeous, gor'jus, *not* gor'je-us.
gosling, gŏz'ling, *not* gawz'ling.
gospel, gŏs'pel, *not* gaws'pel.
got, got, *not* gut.
Gothamite, gō'tham-īt or goth'am-īt.
gouge (*noun and verb*), gowj or gōōj.
gourd, gōrd or gōōrd.
government, guv'ern-ment, *not* guv'er-munt.
governor, guv'ern-ur, *not* guv'nur.

gown, gown, *not* gownd *nor* găoon.
granary, gran′a-rĭ, *not* grān′a-rĭ.
grandmother, grand′mu*th*-er, *not* gran′mu*th*-er. So **grand′fa-ther**, &c.
gratis, grā′tis, *not* grä′tis.
gravel, grav′el, *not* grav′l.
grease (*noun*), grēs, *not* grēz.
grease (*verb*), grēz, *not* grēs. So **greased**, **greas′-ing**, **greas′y**.
grew, grōō, *not* grū.
grievous, grēv′us, *not* grēv′ĭ-us.
grimace, grĭ-māce′, *not* grim′āce.
grimalkin, grĭ-măl′kin, *not* grĭ-mawl′kin.
grimy, grī′mĭ, *not* grĭm′ĭ.
grindstone, grīnd′stōn, *colloquially*, grĭn′stōn.
grisly, griz′lĭ, *not* gris′lĭ.
groat, grawt, *not* grōt.
grovel, grov′l, *not* grov′el.
guardian, gard′ĭ-an, *not* gar-dēn′ *nor* gar′jan.
guava, gwä′va, *not* gwaw′va *nor* gwā′va.
gubernatorial, gu-ber-na-to′rĭ-al, *not* gub-er-na-to′rĭ-al.
guerdon, g̅er′dun, *not* gwer′dun.
guild, g̅ĭld, *not* g̅īld.
guillotine, g̅il-o-tēn′, *not* g̅il′o-tin.
gum′-arabic, gum-ăr′a-bik, *not* gum–a-rā′bik.
gums, gumz, *not* gōōmz.
gunwale, gun′el or gun′wāl.

---

gutta-percha, gut´ta-per´cha, *not* gut´ta-per´ka.
gymnasium, jim-na´zĭ-um or jim-na´zhĭ-um.
gypsy, jip´sĭ, *not* ḡip´sĭ.
gypsum, jip´sum, *not* ḡip´sum.

H.

halcyon, hăl´sĭ-un or hăl´shĭ-un.
half, häf, *not* hăf.
halfpenny, hā´pen-nĭ, häf´pen-nĭ, or hăp´en-nĭ.
halibut, hol´ĭ-but or hăl´ĭ-but. In England the latter is preferred.
halve, häv, *not* hăv.
handbook, hand´bo͝ok, *not* han´bo͝ok.
handful, hand´fo͝ol, *not* han´fo͝ol.
handkerchiefs, hang´ker-chifs, *not* hang´ker-chēvz.
harass, har´as, *not* ha-ras´.
harem, hā´rem, *not* hăr´em.
haslet, hăs´let or hä´slet.
hasten, hās´n, *not* hās´tn.
haunch, hänch, *not* hawnch.
haunt, hänt, *not* hawnt.
heard, herd, *not* hērd.
hearth, härth, *not* herth, except in poetry.
heather, hĕ*th*´er or hēth´er. In Scotland the word is always pronounced hĕ*th*´er.
heaven, hev´n, *not* hev´un.

Hebe, he′be, *not* hēb.
hegira, he-ji′ra or hej′ĭ-ra. In England hej′ĭ-ra is preferred.
height, hīt, *not* hīth.
heinous, hā′nus, *not* hān′yus *nor* he′nus.
heliotrope, hē′lĭ-o-trōp, *not* hel′ĭ-o-trōp.
Hellenic, hel-len′ik or hel-lē′nik.
helot, hel′ot or hē′lot.
hemistich, hem′ĭ-stik, *not* hem′ĭ-stich.
herb, erb or herb. So **herb′age, herb′y.**
herbaceous, her-ba′shus, *not* her-ba′se-us.
Herculean, her-cu′le-an, *not* her-cu-le′an.
hereof, hēr-of′ or hēr-ov′.
herewith, hēr-with′ or hēr-wi*th*′.
heroine, hĕr′o-ĭn, *not* hĕr′o-īn *nor* he′ro-īn.
heroism, hĕr′o-izm, *not* he′ro-izm.
hibernate, hi′ber-nāt, *not* hi-ber′nāt.
hiccough, hik′up or hik′kof.
hideous, hid′e-us, *not* hē′jus *nor* hij′us.
highwayman, hi′wa-man, *not* hi-wa′man.
hilarity, hī-lăr′ĭ-tĭ or hĭ-lăr′ĭ-tĭ. So **hila′rious.**
Hindoo, hin-dōō′ or hin′dōō.
hippopotamus, hip-po-pot′a-mus, *not* hip-po-po-ta′mus.
hirsute, her-sūt′, *not* her′sūt.
history, his′to-rĭ, *not* his′trĭ.
hoist, hoist, *not* hīst.
hollyhock, hol′lĭ-hŏck, *not* hol′lĭ-hawk.

holm, hōm or hōlm.

holocaust, hol'o-kawst, *not* hō'lo-kawst.

homage, hom'āj, *not* om'āj.

homely, hōm'lĭ, *not* hum'lĭ.

homestead, hōm'sted, *not* hōm'stid.

homœopathy, ho-me-op'a-thĭ, *not* ho'me-o-path-ĭ.

homogeneous, ho-mo-je'ne-us, *not* hŏm'o-je-ne-us.

honest, on'est, *not* on'ist.

hoop, hōōp or hŏŏp.

horizon, ho-ri'zun, *not* hor'ĭ-zn.

horrid, hŏr'id, *not* hawr'id. So **hor'ri-ble.**

horseradish, horse'rad-ish, *not* horse'red-ish.

horologe, hor'o-lōj or hor'o-lŏj.

hospitable, hos'pĭ-ta-bl, *not* hos-pit'a-bl.

hospital, hos'pĭ-tal, *not* os'pĭ-tal, *nor* haws'pĭ-tl.

hostage, hŏs'tāj, *not* haws'tāj.

hostile, hos'tīl, *not* hos-tīl *nor* haws'tīl.

hostler, os'ler or hŏs'ler, *not* haws'ler. In England *os'ler* only is approved.

hound, hownd, *not* hown.

housewife, huz'wĭf or hows'wīf. So **house'-wifery.**

hovel, hŏv'el, *not* huv'el.

hover, huv'er, *not* hŏv'er.

humble, hum'bl or um'ble. The latter is preferred in England.

humor, yū'mur or hū'mur. So **hu'morous, hu'-morist.** Smart says, *hu'mor* (in the sense of *moisture or fluid of the animal body*), *ū'mor* (in other senses).

hundred, hun'dred, *not* hun'durd.

hungry, hung'grĭ, *not* hung'ḡer-ĭ.

hurrah, hōōr-rä', *not* hur-raw'.

hussar, hōōz-zar', *not* huz-zar'.

hustle, hus'l, *not* hus'tl.

huswife, huz'if or huz'wĭf.

huzza, hōō-zä', *not* hŭz-ä'.

hydatid, hī'da-tid or hid'a-tid.

hydropathy, hi-drop'a-thĭ, *not* hi'dro-path-ĭ. So **hy-drop'a-thist.**

hygiene, hi'jĭ-ēn or hi'jēn.

hymeneal, hi-me-ne'al, *not* hi-me'ne-al.

hymned, hĭmd or hĭm'ned. So **hym'ning.**

hyperbole, hi-per'bo-le, *not* hi'per-bōl.

hypochondriac, hip-o-kon'drĭ-ak, *not* hi-po-chon'drĭ-ak.

hypocrisy, hĭ-pok'rĭ-sĭ, *not* hī-pok'rĭ-sĭ. So **hy-po-crit'i-cal.**

hypothenuse, hi-poth'e-nūs, *not* hi-poth'e-nūz.

hypothetic, hi-po-thet'ik or hip-o-thet'ik.

hypothetical, hi-po-thet'ik-al, *not* hip-o-thet'ik-al.

hyssop, his'up or hiz'up.

I.

idea, i-de'a, *not* i-de'.
ideal, i-de'al, *not* i-dēl'.
idol, i'dol, *not* i'dl.
idyl, ī'dil, *not* ĭd'il.
ignominious, ig-no-min'ĭ-us, *not* ig-no-min'yus.
ignoramus, ig-no-ra'mus, *not* ig-no-rä'mus.
illusive, il-lu'siv, *not* il-lu'ziv.
illustrate, il-lus'trāt, *not* il'lus-trāt. So **il-lus'-trat-ed, il-lus'tra-tive, il-lus'tra-tor.**
imagery, im'āj-rĭ or im'a-jĕr-ĭ.
imbecile, im-be-sēl', im'be-sĭl, or im-bes'il.
imbrue, im-brōō', *not* im-brū'.
immediate, im-me'dĭ-āt, *not* im-me'jāt.
immortality, im-mor-tal'ĭ-tĭ, *not* im-mer-tal'ĭ-tĭ.
impartiality, im-par-shĭ-al'ĭ-tĭ or im-par-shal'ĭ-tĭ.
impetus, im'pe-tus, *not* im-pe'tus.
impiously, im'pĭ-us-lĭ, *not* im-pī'us-lĭ.
implacable, im-pla'ka-bl, *not* im-plak'a-bl.
importune, im-por-tūn', *not* im-por'tūn.
imposter, im-pŏs'ter, *not* im-paws'ter.
imposthume, im-pŏs'tūm or im-pŏst'hūm.
impotence, im'po-tence, *not* im-po'tence. So **im'po-tent.**
imprimatur, im-prĭ-mā'tur, *not* im-prĭ-mä'tur.
improvise, im-pro-vīz', *not* im'pro-vīz.
inamorata, in-am-o-rä'ta, *not* in-am-o-rā'ta.

inaugurate, in-au′gū-rāt, *not* in-au′gŭr-āt.
inchoate, ing′ko-āt or in′ko-āt.
inchoative, in-ko′a-tĭv, *not* in-cho′a-tĭv.
incisive, in-si′siv, *not* in-si′ziv.
incisor, in-si′sor or in-si′zor.
inclusive, in-klu′siv, *not* in-klu′ziv.
incommensurable, in-kom-men′shōō-ra-bl, *not* in-kom-men′zhōō-ra-bl.
incommensurate, in-kom-men′shōō-rāt, *not* in-kom-men′zhōō-rāt.
incomparable, in-kom′pa-ra-bl, *not* in-kom-pȧr′-a-bl.
inconvenience, in-kon-vēn′yence or in-kon-vē′-nĭ-ence. So **in-con-ven′ient.**
increase (*noun*), in′krēs or in-krēs′.
increment, in′kre-ment or ing′kre-ment.
incubate, in′ku-bāt or ing′ku-bāt.
incubus, in′ku-bus or ing′ku-bus.
indecorus, in-de-ko′rus or in-dek′o-rus.
Indian, ind′yan or in′dĭ-an, *not* in′jun.
indicative,* in-dik′a-tiv, *not* in′dĭ-ka-tiv.
indicatory, in′dĭ-ka-to-rĭ, *not* in-dik′a-to-rĭ.
indigenous, in-dij′e-nus, *not* in-dig̅′e-nus.
indisputable, in-dis′pu-ta-bl, *not* in-dis-pu′ta-bl.
individual, in-dĭ-vid′ū-al, *not* in-dĭ-vid′ōō-al.

* When used in the general sense of *showing* or *pointing out*, Smart pronounces this word *in′di-ca-tive*, but in its grammatical sense he pronounces it *in-dic′a-tive.*

indocile, in-dos'ĭl, *not* in-do'sil.
industry, in'dus-trĭ, *not* in-dus'trĭ.
inertia, in-er'shĭ-a, *not* in-er'sha.
inexhaustible, in-eks-hawst'ĭ-bl, *commonly* in-eks-awst'ĭ-bl.
inexplicable, in-eks'plĭ-ka-bl, *not* in-eks-plik'a-bl.
infamously, in'fa-mus-lĭ, *not* in-fa'mus-lĭ.
infantile, in'fan-tīl or in'fan-tĭl.
infantine, in'fan-tīn or in'fan-tĭn.
inferrible, in-fĕr'rĭ-bl, *not* in-fer'rĭ-bl.
infidel, in'fi-del, *not* in'fi-dl.
ingenious, in-jēn'yus or in-jē'nĭ-us.
ingrate, in'grāt or in-grāt'.
ingratiate, in-gra'shĭ-āt, *not* in-gra'shāt.
ingredient, in-gre'dĭ-ent, *not* in-gre'jent.
inhospitable, in-hos'pĭ-ta-bl, *not* in-hos-pit'a-bl.
inimical, in-im'ĭ-kal; in-ĭ-mi'kal *is obsolescent.*
initiate, in-ĭ'shĭ-āt, *not* in-ĭ'shāt.
innate, in-nāt' or in'nāt.
innocent, in'no-sent, *not* in'no-sunt.
inquiry, in-kwī'rĭ, *not* in'kwĭ-rĭ.
insatiate, in-sā'shĭ-āt, *not* in-sā'shāt. So **in-sa'-ti-a-ble.**
insects, in'sekts, *not* in'seks.
insition, in-sish'un or in-sizh'un.
inspiratory, in-spīr'a-to-rĭ or in'spĭ-ra-to-rĭ.
in statu quo, in sta'tu kwo, *not* in stat'ōō kwo.
instead, in-sted', *not* in-stid'.

instinct (*adj.*), in-stingkt′, *not* in′stingkt.
institute, in′stĭ-tūt, *not* in′stĭ-tōōt. So **in-sti-tu′-tion.**
integer, in′te-jer, *not* in′te-gur.
integral, in′te-gral, *not* in-te′gral. So **in′te-grant.**
intellect, in′tel-lekt, *not* in′tŭ-lekt. So **in-tel-lect′u-al.**
intercalary, in-ter′kal-a-rĭ, *not* in-ter-kal′a-rĭ.
interest, in′ter-est, *not* in′trest *nor* (*verb*) in-ter-est′.
interested, in′ter-est-ed, *not* in-ter-est′ed.
interesting, in′ter-est-ing, *not* in-ter-est′ing.
interlocutor, in-ter-lok′u-tur, *not* in-ter-lo-ku′tur.
international, in-ter-nash′un-al, *not* in-ter-nā′-shun-al.
internecine, in-ter-ne′sīn, *not* in-ter-ne′sĭn.
interpolate, in-ter′po-lāt, *not* in-ter-po′lāt.
interstice, in′ter-stĭs or in-ter′stĭs.
intestine, in-tes′tĭn, *not* in-tes′tīn.
intrigue (*noun and verb*), in-trēg′, *not* in′trēg.
intrude, in-trōōd′, *not* in-trūd′.
intrusive, in-trōō′siv, *not* in-trōō′ziv.
inure, in-yōōr′, *not* in-ōōr′.
invalid (*noun*), in′va-lid or in-va-lēd′.
invasive, in-va′siv, *not* in-va′ziv.
inveigle, in-ve′gl, *not* in-va′gl.
inventory, in′ven-to-rĭ, *not* in-ven′to-rĭ.
involucre, in-vo-lu′ker, *not* in′vo-lu-ker.
iodide, i′o-dĭd or i′o-dīd.

iodine, ī'o-dĭn or ī'o-dīn, *not* ī'o-dēn.
irate, i-rāt', *not* ī'rāt.
iron, ī'urn, *not* ī'run.
irrational, ĭr-rash'un-al, *not* ĭr-rā'shun-al.
irrefragable, ĭr-ref'ra-ga-bl, *not* ĭr-re-fra'ga-bl.
irrefutable, ĭr-ref'u-ta-bl or ĭr-re-fū'ta-bl.
irreparable, ĭr-rep'a-ra-bl, *not* ĭr-re-pår'a-bl.
irrevocable, ĭr-rev'o-ka-bl, *not* ir-re-vo'ka-bl.
isochronal, ī-sok'ro-nal, *not* ī-so-kro'nal.
isolate, iz'o-lāt or is'o-lāt, *not* ī'so-lāt. So **is-o-la'tion.**
isosceles, ī-sos'se-lēz, *not* ī-sos'lêz.
isothermal, ī-so-therm'al, *not* is'o-therm-al.
issue, ish'o͞o or ish'yo͞o.
isthmus, ist'mus or is'mus.
Italian, ĭ-tal'yan, *not* ī-tal'yan.
italic, ĭ-tal'ik, *not* ī-tal'ik.
ivory, ī'vo-rĭ, *not* īv'rĭ.

J.

jackal, jak'awl, *not* jak'ăl.
jaguar, jag-u-ar', *not* jag-wär' *nor* jā'gwär.
jalap, jăl'ap, *not* jol'ap.
January, jan'u-a-rĭ, *not* jen'u-a-rĭ.
jasmine, jaz'min or jas'min.
jaundice, jän'dĭs, *not* jawn'dĭs.
jaunt, jänt, *not* jawnt.

javelin, jăv′lin, *not* jăv′e-lin.
jejune, je-jo͞on′ or je-jūn′.
jewsharp, jūz′harp, *not* jūs′harp.
jocose, jo-kōs′, *not* jok-ōs′ *nor* jo-kōz′.
jocund, jok′und, *not* jo′kund.
joist, joist, *not* jīst.
jonquille, jon′kwil or jung′kwil.
jostle, jos′l, *not* jos′tl. So **jost′ling.**
joust, just, *not* jo͞ost *nor* jowst.
jovial, jo′vĭ-al, *not* jōv′yal.
jowl, jōl, *not* jowl.
jugular, ju′gu-lar, *not* jug′u-lar.
jujube, ju′jūb, *not* ju′ju-be.
junior, jūn′yur or ju′nĭ-ur.
just, just, *not* jest.
justificative, jus′tĭ-fĭ-ka-tĭv or jus-tif′ĭ-ka-tĭv.
justificatory, jus′tif-ĭ-ka-to-rĭ or jus-tif′ĭ-ka-to-rĭ.
juvenile, ju′ve-nĭl, *not* ju′ve-nīl.

K.

keelson, kĕl′sun or kēl′sun.
kept, kept, *not* kep.
kettle, ket′tl, *not* kit′tl.
khan (*a Tartar chief*), kawn or kăn.
kiln, kil, *not* kiln.
kindness, kīnd′nes, *not* kīn′nes.
kitchen, kitch′en, *not* kitch′n *nor* kitch′ing.

L.

label, la'bel, *not* la'bl.
laboratory, lab'or-a-to-rĭ, *not* la-bor'a-to-rĭ.
laborer, la'bor-er, *not* la'brur.
lachrymose, lak'rĭ-mōs or lak-rĭ-mōs'.
lackadaisical, lak-a-da'zik-al, *not* lak-a-da'sik-al.
lamentable, lam'en-ta-bl, *not* la-ment'a-bl.
landau, lan'daw or lan-daw'.
landlord, land'lord, *not* lan'lurd.
lang-syne, läng-sīn', *not* lang-zīn'.
language, lang'gwāj, *not* lan'gwāj. So **lan'guid**, **lan'guish.**
languor, lang'gwur, *not* lan'gwur.
laniate, lā'nĭ-āt or lăn'ĭ-āt.
lapel, la-pel', *not* lap-el'.
larum, lăr'um, *not* lär'um.
laryngeal, lăr-in-je'al or la-rin'je-al.
larynx, lăr'inks, *not* lär'inks *nor* lā'rinks.
latent, lā'tent, *not* lăt'ent.
lath (*noun and verb*), läth, *not* lä*th*; (*noun pl.*) **laths**, lä*thz*, *not* läths.
lathe, lā*th*, *not* lä*th*.
Latin, lat'in, *not* lat'n.
laudanum, law'da-num or lŏd'a-num, *not* lod'num.
laugh, läf, *not* lăf.
launch, länch, *not* lănch *nor* lawnch.
laundry, län'drĭ, *not* lawn'drĭ. So **laun'dress.**

laurel, law′rel or lŏr′el.
lava, lā′va or lä′va.
leaped, lēpt or lĕpt.
learned (*adj.*), lern′ed, *not* lernd *nor* lun′ed.
leeward, lē′ward or lōō′urd.
legate, leg′āt, *not* le′gāt.
legend, lej′end or le′jend.
legendary, lĕj′en-da-rĭ, *not* lē′jen-da-rĭ.
legislative, lej′is-la-tĭv, *not* lej-is-la′tĭv *nor* le-jis′-la-tĭv.
legislature, lej′is-lāt-yur, *not* lej-is-lāt′yur *nor* le-jis′la-tūr.
legume, leg′ūm or le-gūm′.
leisure, lē′zhur, *not* lĕzh′ur *nor* lā′zhur.
lenient, le′nĭ-ent, *not* len′ĭ-ent.
lenitive, len′i-tĭv, *not* le′ni-tĭv.
leper, lep′er, *not* le′per.
lessor, les′sor or les-sor′.
lethargic, le-thar′jik, *not* leth′ar-jik.
lettuce, let′tis, *not* let′tōōs *nor* let′tus.
levantine, le-van′tĭn or lev′an-tĭn.
levee, lev′e. In the United States, when used in the sense of an assembly of visitors, it is usually pronounced le-ve′.
level, lev′el, *not* lev′l.
lever, lē′ver or lev′er.
Leyden-jar, lī′dn-jar or lā′dn-jar.
libel, li′bel, *not* li′bl.

libertine, lib′er-tĭn, *not* lib′er-tīn.
library, lī′bra-rĭ, *not* lī′brĭ.
licentiate, li-sen′shĭ-āt, *not* li-sen′shăt.
lichen, lī′ken or lich′en.
licorice, lik′o-ris, *not* lik′er-ish.
lien, lē′en or lī′en, *not* lēn.
lieutenant, lu-ten′ant or lev-ten′ant.
lilac, lī′lak, *not* lī′lok *nor* la′lok.
lineament (*a feature*), lin′e-a-ment, *not* lin′e-ment.
To be distinguished from **lin′i-ment** (*an ointment*).
liquor, lik′ur, *not* lik′wur.
listen, lis′n, *not* lis′tn.
literati, lit-er-a′tī, *not* lit-er-ä′tī.
lithe, līth, *not* līth. So **lithe′some.**
lithography, lith-og′ra-fĭ, *not* lī-thog′ra-fĭ *nor* lith′o-graf-ĭ. So **lith-og′ra-pher.**
little, lit′tl, *not* lē′tl.
litre [Fr.], le′ter or lī′ter.
livelong, lĭv′long, *not* līv′long.
livery, lĭv′er-ĭ, *not* līv′er-ĭ.
livre [Fr.], le′ver or lī′ver.
llama, la′ma or lä′ma.
loath (*adj.*), lōth, *not* lō*th* *nor* lawth.
loathsome, lō*th*′sum, *not* lōth′sum.
locust, lo′kust, *not* lo′kus.
long-lived, long′-līvd, *not* long′-lĭvd.
lord, lord, *not* lawurd.
loyal, loi′al, *not* law′yal.

lucid, lū'sid, *not* lōō'sid.
lucre, lū'kur, *not* lōō'kur.
ludicrous, lū'dĭ-krus, *not* lōō'dĭ-krus.
lure, lūr, *not* lōōr.
lurid, lū'rid, *not* lōō'rid.
lute, lūt, *not* lōōt.
luxurious, lugz-ū'rĭ-us or luks-ū'rĭ-us. So **luxu'riant, luxu'riate.**
luxury, luks'u-rĭ, *not* lugz'u-rĭ.
lyceum, li-se'um, *not* li'se-um.

M.

Machiavelian, mak-ĭ-a-vel'yan, *not* mach'ĭ-a-velyan.
machination, mak-ĭ-na'shun, *not* mach-ĭ-na'shun.
Madeira, ma-de'ra or ma-da'ra.
magazine, mag-a-zēn', *not* mag'a-zēn.
magnesia, mag-ne'zhĭ-a or mag-ne'zha.
magnolia, mag-no'lĭ-a, *not* mag-nōl'ya.
maintain, mān-tān' or men-tān'.
maintenance, mān'ten-ance, *not* mān-tān'ance.
malaria, ma-la'rĭ-a, *not* ma-lä'rĭ-a.
malefactor, măl-e-fak'tur or mal'e-fak-tur.
malinger, ma-ling'gur, *not* ma-lin'jur.
mamma, mam-mä', *not* mam'mä.
mammillary, mam'mil-la-rĭ, *not* ma-mil'la-rĭ.
mandarin, man-da-rēn', *not* man'da-rĭn.

manes (*L. pl.*), ma'nēz, *not* mānz.
manganese, mang-ga-nēz', *not* man'ga-nēs.
manger, mān'jer, *not* măn'jer.
mangy, mān'gĭ, *not* măn'jĭ.
mania, ma'nĭ-a, *not* mān'ya.
maniacal, ma-ni'a-kal, *not* ma'nĭ-ak-al.
manœuvre, ma-nōō'ver, *not* ma-nū'ver.
Mansard-roof, man'sard-rōōf, *not* man-sard'-rōōf.
mantua-maker, man'tu-a-ma'ker or man'tu-ma'-ker.
marasmus, ma-raz'mus, *not* ma-ras'mus.
marigold, măr'i-gōld, *not* mā'rĭ-gōōld.
marital, măr'i-tal, *not* mär'i-tal.
maritime, măr'ĭ-tĭm, *not* măr'ĭ-tīm.
market, mar'ket, *not* mar'kit.
marvel, mar'vel, *not* mar'vl.
masculine, mas'ku-lĭn, *not* mas'ku-līn.
massacred, mas'sa-kerd, *not* mas'sa-krēd.
massacring, mas'sa-kring, *not* mas'sa-ker-ing.
master, mas'ter, *not* mos'ter.
matin, mat'in, *not* ma'tin.
matrice (*a womb*), ma'trĭs; (*a mould*), mat'rĭs.
matrix, ma'triks, *not* mat'riks.
matron, ma'tron, *not* mat'ron.
matronal, ma'tron-al or mat'ron-al.
mattress, mat'tres, *not* ma'tras.
matutinal, mat'u-tī-nal or mat-u-tī'nal, *not* ma-tu'ti-nal.

mausoleum, maw-so-le'um, *not* maw-so'le-um.
measure, mezh'ur, *not* māzh'ur.
mechanist, mek'an-ist, *not* me-kan'ist.
medal, med'al, *not* med'l.
medicinal, me-dis'in-al, *not* med-ĕ-sī'nal.
mediæval, me-dĭ-e'val, *not* med-ĭ-e'val.
medicine, med'ĭ-sin, *not* med'sun.
mediocre, me'dĭ-o-ker, *not* me-dĭ-o'ker.
medium, me'dĭ-um, *not* me'jum.
meerschaum, mēr'shawm or mēr'showm, *not* mēr'shum.
meliorate, mēl'yo-rāt or me'lĭ-o-rāt.
mellow, mel'low, *not* mel'ler.
melodeon, me-lo'de-on, *not* mel-o-de'on.
melodrama, mel-o-dra'ma, *not* mel-o-drä'ma.
memoir, mem'wor or mēm'wor.
memory, mem'o-rĭ, *not* mem'rĭ.
menagerie, men-äzh'er-ĭ or men-ăzh'er-ĭ.
mensurable, men'shōō-ra-bl, *not* men'zhōō-ra-bl.
mensuration, men-shōō-ra'shun, *not* men-zhōō-ra'shun.
mercantile, mer'kan-tĭl or mer'kan-tīl, *not* mer'-kan-tēl.
mesmerize, mez'mer-īz, *not* mes'mer-īz. So **mesmer'ic, mes'mer-ism.**
metal, met'al or met'l.
metamorphose, met-a-mor'fōs, *not* met-a-mor'fōz.
metonymy, me-ton'ĭ-mĭ or met'o-nim-ĭ.

metropolitan, met-ro-pol′i-tan, *not* me-tro-pol′i-tan.
mezzotint, med′zo-tint or met′zo-tint.
miasma, mī-az′ma, *not* me-az′ma.
Michælmas, mĭk′el-mas, *not* mī′kel-mas.
microscope, mi′kro-skōp, *not* mik′ro-skōp. So **mi-cro-scop′ic, mi′cro-sco-pist.**
midwifery, mid′wĭf-rĭ or mid′wīf-rĭ.
milch, mĭlch, *not* mĭlks.
mineralogy, min-er-ăl′o-jĭ, *not* min-er-ol′o-jĭ.
miniature, min′ĭ-tūr or min′ĭ-a-tūr.
minotaur, min′o-tawr, *not* mi′no-tawr.
minus, mi′nus, *not* mĭn′us.
minute (*adj.*), mĭ-nūt′ or mī-nūt′.
minute (*noun*), min′it or min′ūt.
miracle, mĭr′a-kl, *not* mĕr′a-kl.
miraculous, mĭ-rak′u-lus, *not* mī-rak′u-lus.
misanthrope, mis′an-thrōp, *not* miz′an-thrōp *nor* mis-an′thrōp.
mischievous, mis′chĭv-us, *not* mis-chēv′us.
misconstrue, mis-kon′strōō, *not* mis-kon-strōō′.
misery, miz′er-ĭ, *not* miz′rĭ.
misogynist, mĭ-soj′ĭ-nist, *not* mī-sog′ĭ-nist.
mistletoe, miz′l-tō, *not* mis′l-tō.
mitten, mit′ten, *not* mit′n.
mobile, mo′bĭl or mob′ĭl.
model, mod′el, *not* mod′l.
modest, mod′est, *not* mod′ist.

moiety, moi′e-tĭ or maw′e-tĭ.
moisten, mois′n, *not* mois′tn.
molecular, mo-lek′u-lar, *not* mo′le-ku-lar.
molecule, mŏl′e-kūl, *not* mōl′kūl *nor* mō′le-kūl.
mollient, mol′yent or mol′lĭ-ent.
momentary, mo′ment-a-rĭ, *not* mo-ment′a-rĭ.
monad, mon′ad, *not* mo′nad.
monetary, mun′e-ta-rĭ or mon′e-ta-rĭ.
mongrel, mung′grel, *not* mon′grel.
monogram, mon′o-gram, *not* mo′no-gram.
monograph, mon′o-graf, *not* mo′no-graf.
monomania, mon-o-ma′nĭ-a, *not* mo-no-ma′nĭ-a. So **mon-o-ma′ni-ac.**
monument, mon′u-ment, *not* mon′i-ment.
morale, mo-räl′, *not* mo-rāl′.
morphine, mor′fĭn, *not* mor′fēn.
morsel, mor′sel, *not* mor′sl.
mortal, mor′tal, *not* mor′tl.
Moslem, moz′lem, *not* mos′lem.
moss,[4] moss, *not* maws. So **moss′y.**
moth,[4] moth, *not* mo*th*.
moths,[4] mo*th*s, *not* moths.
mountain, mown′tin, *not* mown′ting *nor* mown′tn.
mountainous, mown′tin-us, *not* mown-tān′ĭ-us.
mouths (*n. pl.*), mow*thz*, *not* mowths.
multiplicand, mul-tĭ-plĭ-kand,′ *not* mul′tĭ-plĭ-kand.
multiplication, mul-tĭ-plĭ-ka′shun, *not* mul-tĭ-pĭ-ka′shun.

municipal, mu-nis′ĭ-pal, *not* mu′nĭ-sip-al.
murderer, mur′der-er, *not* mur′drer.
muscovado, mus-ko-vā′do, *not* mus-ko-vä′do.
museum, mu-ze′um, *not* mu′ze-um.
mushroom, mush′rōōm, *not* mush′rōōn.
mustache, mus-täsh′, *not* mus′tăsh *nor* mus-tāsh′.
myrmidon, mur′mĭ-don, *not* mĭr′mĭ-don.
mythology, mĭ-thol′o-jĭ, *not* mī-thol′o-jĭ.

N.

naiad, nā′yad or nā′ad.
naïve, nä′ēv, *not* nāv.
naïvely, nä′ēv-lĭ or nāv′lĭ.
naïveté, nä′ēv-tā, *not* nāv′te.
naked, na′ked, *not* nek′ed.
nape, nāp, *not* năp.
naphtha, nap′tha or naf′tha.
narrate, năr-rāt′ or năr′rāt, *not* när-rāt′.
narrow, năr′ro, *not* när′ro.
nasal, na′zal, *not* na′sal.
nascent, năs′sent, *not* nā′sent.
national, nash′un-al, *not* na′shun-al. So **na-tion-al′i-ty**.
nature, nāt′yur, *not* nā′tur.
nausea, naw′she-a, *not* naw′se-a. So **nau′se-ate**.
nauseous, naw′shus, *not* naw′se-us.
nearest, nēr′est, *not* nēr′ist.

'neath, nē*th*, *not* nēth.

necrology, ne-krol'o-jĭ, *not* nek-rōl'o-jĭ. So **necrol'o-gist.**

nectarine, nek'ta-rĭn, *not* nek'ta-rīn *nor* nek'ta-rēn.

ne'er, nâr, *not* nēr.

negotiate, ne-go'shĭ-āt, *not* ne-go'shāt. So **ne-go'ti-a-ble, ne-go-ti-a'tion.**

negro, ne'gro, *not* nig'ro.

neighboring, na'bur-ing, *not* na'bring.

neither, nē'*th*er, or nī'*th*er.

nephew, nev'yōō or nef'yōō.

nepotism, nĕp'o-tizm, *not* nē'po-tizm.

nescience, nesh'ĭ-ence or nesh'ence.

nestle, nes'l, *not* nes'tl.

nethermost, ne*th*'er-mōst, *not* neth'er-mōst.

neuralgia, nu-ral'jĭ-a, *not* nu-ral'jĭ *nor* nu-ral'ĭ-jĭ.

neuter, nū'ter, *not* nōō'ter.

neutral, nū'tral, *not* nōō'tral.

new, nū, *not* nōō.

newspaper, nūz'pa-per, *not* nōōs'pa-per.

nicety, nī'sĭ-tĭ, *not* nīs'tĭ.

nickel, nik'el, *not* nik'l.

nicotine, nik'o-tĭn, *not* nik'o-tēn.

nomad, nom'ad, *not* no'mad.

nomenclature, no'men-klāt-yur or no-men-klāt'-yur.

nominative, nom'ĭ-na-tĭv, *not* nom'na-tĭv.

none, nun, *not* nōn.
nook, nŏŏk or nŏŏk.
noose, nōōz or nōōs.
nosology, no-sol′o-jĭ or no-zol′o-jĭ.
notable *(remarkable)*, nōt′a-bl; *(careful and bustling)*, nŏt′-a-bl.
nothing, nŭth′ing, *not* nŏth′ing.
novel, nov′el, *not* nov′l.
novitiate, no-vĭsh′ĭ-āt, *not* no-vĭ′shāt.
nuisance, nū′sance, *not* nōō′sance.
numerous, nu′mer-ous, *not* nōōm′rus.
numismatics, nu-miz-mat′iks, *not* nu-mis-mat′iks.
nuncio, nun′shĭ-o, *not* nun′sho *nor* nun′sĭ-o.
nuncupative, nun-ku′pa-tiv or nun′ku-pa-tiv. So **nun-cu-pa-to-ry.**
nuptial, nup′shal, *not* nup′chal.
nutriment, nū′trĭ-ment, *not* nōō′trĭ-ment. So **nu-tri′tious, nu-tri′tion, nu′tri-tive.**

O.

oasis, o′a-sis or o-ā′sis.
oath, ōth, *not* ō*th*.
oaths, ō*th*z, *not* ōths.
obdurate, ob′du-rāt or ob-du′rāt. So **ob-du-ra-cy.**
obeisance, o-bā′sance or o-bē′sance. So **o-bei′-sant.**

obese, o-bēs′, *not* o-bēz′.
obesity, o-bĕs′ĭ-tĭ, *not* o-be′sĭ-tĭ.
obey, o-bā′, *not* ŭ-bā′.
objurgate, ob-jur′gāt, *not* ob′jur-gāt.
obligatory, ob′lĭ-ga-to-rĭ, *not* ob-lig′a-to-rĭ.
oblige, o-blīj′, *not* o-blēj′.
oblique, ob-lēk′ or ob-līk′.
obscenity, ob-sen′ĭ-tĭ, *not* ob-sēn′ĭ-tĭ.
obsequies, ob′se-kwiz, *not* ob-se′kwiz.
obsolete, ob′so-lēt, *not* ob-so-lēt′.
obtrude, ob-trōōd′, *not* ob-trūd′.
obtrusion, ob-trōō′zhun, *not* ob-trū′zhun.
obtrusive, ob-trōō′siv, *not* ob-trōō′ziv.
occult, ok-kult′, *not* ok′kult.
oceanic, o-she-an′ik, *not* o-shan′ik *nor* o-se-an′ik.
octavo, ok-tā′vo, *not* ok-tä′vo.
octogenary, ok-toj′e-na-rĭ or ok′to-je-na-rĭ.
Odeon, o-de′on, *not* o′de-on.
odious, o′dĭ-us, *not* o′jus.
Odyssey, od′is-se, *not* o-dis′ĭ.
off,[4] off, *not* awf.
offal,[4] of′fal, *not* aw′fl.
offer,[4] of′fer, *not* aw′fer.
office,[4] of′fis, *not* aw′fis.
officiate, of-fish′ĭ-āt, *not* of-fish′āt.
officinal, of-fĭ-si′nal or of-fis′ĭ-nal.
offspring,[4] of′spring, *not* awf′spring.
oft,[4] oft, *not* awft.

often,[4] of'n, *not* of'ten *nor* awf'tn.
ogle, o'gl, *not* og'l.
old, ōld, *not* ōl.
olden, ōld'n, *not* ōld'en.
olefiant, o'le-fi-ant or o-lef'ĭ-ant.
olibanum, o-lib'a-num or ol-ĭ-bā'num.
olio, o'lĭ-o or ōl'yo.
omega, o-me'ga or o-meg'a.
omelet, om'e-let or om'let.
ominous, om'in-us, *not* o'min-us.
omniscient, om-nish'ĭ-ent or om-nish'ent. So **om-nis'cience.**
once, wuns, *not* wunst.
onerous, on'er-us, *not* o'ner-us.
only, ōn'lĭ, *not* un'lĭ.
onyx, ō'niks, *not* ŏn'iks.
ophthalmic, op-thal'mik or of-thal'mik.
opinion, o-pin'yun, *not* ŭ-pin'yun.
opodeldoc, op-o-del'dok or o-po-del'dok, *not* o-po-dil'dok.
opponent, op-po'nent, *not* op'po-nent.
opportunity, op-por-tū'nĭ-tĭ, *not* op-por-tōō'nĭ-tĭ.
or, or, *not* ur.
orange, or'enj, *not* ornj.
orang-outang, o-rang'-ōō-tang', *not* o'rang-ow'-tang.
orchestra, or'kes-tra or or-kes'tra.
orchestral, or'kes-tral, *not* or-kes'tral.

ordeal, or′de-al, *not* or-de′al.
ordinary, or′di-na-rĭ, *not* ord′na-rĭ.
orgies, or′jĭz, *not* or′jēz.
Orion, o-ri′un, *not* o′rĭ-un.
orison, or′ĭ-zun, *not* or′ĭ-sun.
ornate, or′nāt, *not* or-nāt′.
orotund, o′ro-tund, *not* or′o-tund.
Orphean, or-fe′an or or′fe-an.
orthoepy, or′tho-e-pĭ, *not* or-tho′e-pĭ. So **or′-tho-e-pists.**
ostentatious, os-ten-ta′shus, *not* aws-ten-ta′shus.
ostrich, os′trich, *not* os′trij *nor* aws′trich.
ought, awt, *not* ort.
oust, owst, *not* ōōst.
overseer, o-ver-sēr′, *not* o′ver-sēr.
overt, o′vert, *not* o-vert′.
overthrew, o-ver-thrōō′, *not* o-vēr-thrū′.
oyer, o′yer, *not* oi′er.
oxide, oks′ĭd, *not* oks′īd.

P.

pacification, pa-sĭf-ĭ-ka′shun or pas-ĭ-fĭ-ka′shun.
pacificator, pa-sĭf-ĭ-ka′tur or pas-ĭ-fĭ-ka′tur.
pageant, paj′ent or pa′jent. So **pag′eant-ry.**
palace, pal′ăs or pal′ās.
palaver, pa-lä′ver, *not* pa-lav′er.
Palestine, pal′es-tīn, *not* pal′es-tĭn.

palfrey, pawl'frĭ or păl'frĭ.
palliative, pal'lĭ-a-tiv, *not* pal'a-tiv.
palm, päm, *not* păm.
palmy, päm'ĭ, *not* păm'ĭ *nor* păl'mĭ.
palsied, pawl'zid, *not* păl'zid.
paltry, pawl'trĭ, *not* păl'trĭ.
Pandoor, pan'do͞or or pan-do͞or'.
panegyric, pan-e-jĭr'ik or pan-e-jĕr'ik.
pannier, pan'yer or pan'nĭ-er.
panorama, pan-o-rā'ma or pan-o-rä'ma.
pantaloons, pan-ta-lo͞onz', *not* pan'ta-lo͞onz.
Pantheon, pan-the'on or pan'the-on.
pantomime, pan'to-mīm, *not* pan'to-mīn.
papa, pä-pä', *not* pä'pä.
parachute, păr'a-sho͞ot or păr-a-sho͞ot'.
paraffine, păr'a-fīn or păr'af-fīn, *not* păr'af-fēn.
parallelopiped, păr-al-lel-o-pi'ped, *not* păr-al-lel-o-pip'ed.
parcel, par'sel, *not* par'sl.
paregoric, păr-e-gŏr'ik, *not* păr-e-gawr'ik.
parent, pȧr'ent, *not* pā'rent *nor* păr'ent. So **par'-ent-age.**
parhelion, par-he'lĭ-un or par-hēl'yun.
Pariah, pär'ĭ-ah or pā'rĭ-ah.
Parisian, pa-riz'yan or pa-rizh'ĭ-an.
Parmesan, par-me-zan', *not* par-me'san.
parquet, par-kā' or par-ket'.
partiality, par-shĭ-al'ĭ-tĭ, *not* par-shal'ĭ-tĭ.

participle, par′tĭ-sip-l, *not* part′sip-l.
partisan, par′tĭ-zan, *not* par-tĭ-zan′.
partner, part′ner, *not* pard′ner.
partridge, pär′trij, *not* păt′rij.
pastime,[1] pas′tīm, *not* pas′tĭm.
patent, pat′ent or pa′tent.
path, päth, *not* pä*th* nor pă*th*; (*pl.*) pä*th*z, *not* päths *nor* păths.
pathos, pa′thos, *not* păth′os.
patois, pat′waw, *not* pat′woi.
patrimony, pat′rĭ-mo-nĭ, *not* pa′trĭ-mo-nĭ.
patriot, pa′trĭ-ot, *not* păt′rĭ-ot. So **pa-tri-ot′ic.**
patriotism, pa′trĭ-ot-izm, *not* păt′rĭ-ot-izm.
patron, pa′tron, *not* păt′ron.
patronize, pat′ron-īz or pa′tron-īz. So **patron-age, patron-al.**
paunch, pänch or pawnch.
peculiar, pe-kūl′yar or pe-ku′lĭ-ar.
peculiarity, pe-kūl-ĭ-ăr′ĭ-tĭ or pe-kūl-yăr′ĭ-tĭ.
pecuniary, pe-kūn′ya-rĭ or pe-ku′nĭ-a-rĭ.
pedagogism, ped′a-gog-izm, *not* ped′a-go-jizm.
pedagogy, ped′a-go-jĭ or ped a-gŏj-ĭ.
pedal (*adj.*), pe′dal, *not* ped′al.
pedal (*noun*), ped′al, *not* pe′dal.
pedestal, ped′es-tal, *not* pe-des′tal.
pellucid, pel-lū′sid, *not* pel-lōō′sid.
penance, pen′ance, *not* pe′nance.
pencil, pen′sil, *not* pens′l.

penitentiary, pen-e-ten'sha-rĭ, *not* pen-e-ten'shĭ-a-rĭ.
penult, pe'nult or pe-nult'.
peradventure, pĕr-ad-vent'yur, *not* pur-ad-vent'-yur.
peremptory, pĕr'em-to-rĭ, *not* pe-rem'to-rĭ.
perfect (*verb*), per'fekt or per-fekt'.
perfume (*noun*), per'fūm or per-fūm'.
perfume (*verb*), per-fūm', *not* per'fūm.
perfunctory, per-funk'to-rĭ or per'funk-to-rĭ.
perhaps, per-haps', *not* praps *nor* pre-haps'.
periodic, pē-rĭ-od'ik, *not* pĕr-ĭ-od'ik.
periphrasis, pe-rif'ra-sis, *not* pĕr-ĭ-fra'sis.
permit (*noun*), per'mit or per-mit'.
Persian, per'shan, *not* per'zhan.
persuasive, per-swa'siv, *not* per-swa'ziv.
peruke, pĕr'o͝ok, *not* pe-ro͞ok'.
peruse, pe-ro͞oz', *not* pe-rūz'.
pestle, pes'l or pes'tl.
petal, pet'al or pe'tal.
petrel, pet'rel, *not* pe'trel.
pewit, pe'wit, *not* pu'it.
phaeton, fa'e-ton, *not* fe'ton.
phalanx, fa'lanks or fal'anks.
pharmaceutic, far-ma-su'tik, *not* far-ma-ku'tĭk. So **phar-ma-ceu'tist**.
pharmacopœia, far-ma-ko-pe'ya, *not* far-ma-ko'-pe-a.

philanthropy, fĭ-lan'thro-pĭ, *not* fī-lan'thro-pĭ. So **phi-lan'thro-pist, phil-an-throp'ic.**
Philistine, fĭ-lis'tĭn, *not* fil'is-tĭn.
philology, fĭ-lol'o-jĭ, *not* fī-lol'o-jĭ. So **phi-lol'o-gist.**
philosophy, fĭ-los'o-fĭ, *not* fī-los'o-fĭ. So **phi-los'o-pher.**
phonics, fon'iks, *not* fo'niks.
phosphorus, fos'fo-rus, *not* fos-fo'rus.
photographist, fo-tog'ra-fist, *not* fo'to-graf-ist. So **pho-tog'ra-pher.**
phrenologic, fren-o-loj'ik, *not* fre-no-loj'ik.
phthisis, thi'sis or ti'sis.
physiognomy, fiz-ĭ-og'no-mĭ, *not* fiz-ĭ-on'o-mĭ.
pianist, pĭ-ä'nist, *not* pī-an'ist *nor* pe-an'ist *nor* pe'an-ist.
piano, pĭ-ä'no or pe-an'o.
piano-forte, pĭ-ä'no-fōr'te. The pronunciation pĭ-an'o-fōrt, so often heard, is not sanctioned by the orthoëpists.
piazza, pĭ-az'za, *not* pī-az'za.
pibroch, pe'brok or pĭ'brok.
pigeon, pij'un, *not* pij'in.
pilaster, pĭ-las'ter, *not* pil'as-ter.
pincers, pin'serz, *not* pin'cherz unless spelled *pin-* [*chers.*
pinchbeck, pinch'bek, *not* pinch'bak.
piony, pi'o-nĭ, *not* pi'nĭ; but **pe'o-ny** is a better spelling and pronunciation.

piquant, pik′ant or pe′kant.
pismire, piz′mīr or pis′mīr.
pith, pith, *not* peth.
placable, pla′ka-bl, *not* plak′a-bl.
placard (*noun and verb*), pla-kard′, *not* plak′ard.
plagiarism, pla′jĭ-a-rizm or pla′ja-rizm. So **pla′-giary.**
plague, plāg, *not* pleg.
plaintiff, plān′tif, *not* plan′tif.
plait, plāt, *not* plēt.
plateau, plä-to′, *not* plăt-o′.
platina, plat′ĭ-na or pla-te′na.
platinum, plat′ĭ-num or pla-tī′num.
plebeian, ple-be′yan, *not* ple′be-an.
Pleiades, ple′ya-dēz, *not* plī′a-dēz.
plenary, ple′na-rĭ or plen′a-rĭ.
plenipotentiary, plen-ĭ-po-ten′shĭ-a-rĭ or plen-ĭ-po-ten′sha-rĭ.
plenitude, plen′ĭ-tūd, *not* plen′ĭ-tōōd.
plethora, pleth′o-ra, *not* ple-tho′ra.
plethoric, ple-thor′ik or pleth′o-rik.
poignant, poin′ant, *not* poin′yant. So **poign′-an-cy.**
poison, poi′zn, *not* pī′zn.
police, po-lēs′, *not* plēs.
polonaise, pō-lo-nāz′, *not* pŏl-o-nāz′.
polype, pol′ip or pol′i-pe.
pomade, po-mād′, *not* po-mäd′.

poniard, pon'yard, *not* poin'yard.
porcelain, por'se-lān or pors'lin, *not* pōrs'lin.
porch, pōrch, *not* pawrch.
portent, por-tent', *not* pōr'tent.
port-folio, pōrt-fo'lĭ-o or pōrt fōl'yo.
portrait, pōr'trāt, *not* pŏr'trāt. So **por'trait-ure.**
position, po-zish'un, *not* pŭ-zish'un.
possess, poz-zes', *not* pos-ses'. So **pos-ses'sive, pos-ses'sion,** &c.
posterior, pŏs-te'rĭ-ur, *not* pōs-te'rĭ-ur.
posthumous, pŏst'hu-mus, *not* pōst'hu-mus.
potable, po'ta-bl, *not* pot'a-bl.
potato, pō-ta'to, *not* pŭ-ta'to.
potentate, po'ten-tāt, *not* pot'en-tāt.
potentiality, po-ten-shĭ-al'ĭ-tĭ, *not* po-ten-shal'ĭ-tĭ.
prairie, prā'rĭ, *not* per-a'rĭ.
prebend, preb'end, *not* pre'bend.
precedence, pre-sēd'ence, *not* pres'-e-dence.
precedent (*adj.*), pre-sēd'ent, *not* pres'e-dent; (*noun*), pres'e-dent, *not* pre-se'dent.
precept, pre'sept, *not* pres'ept.
preceptory, pre-sep'to-rĭ or pres'ep-to-rĭ.
precise, pre-sīs', *not* pre-sīz'. So **pre-cise'ly.**
predatory, pred'a-to-rĭ, *not* pre'da-to-rĭ.
predecessor, pred-e-ses'sur, *not* pre'de-ses-sur *nor* pred'e-ses-sur.
predilection, pre-dĭ-lek'shun, *not* pred-ĭ-lek'shun *nor* pre-dĭ-lik'shun.

preface (*noun and verb*), pref'ace, *not* pre'face.
prefect, pre'fekt, *not* pref'ekt.
preferment, pre-fer'ment, *not* pref'er-ment.
prehensile, pre-hen'sĭl, *not* pre-hen'sīl.
prelacy, prel'a-sĭ, *not* pre'la-sĭ.
prelate, prel'ăt, *not* pre'lāt.
prelude (*noun*), prel'ūd or pre'lūd.
premier, pre'mĭ-er or prēm'yer.
preposterous, pre-pos'ter-us, *not* pre-pos'trus.
presage (*noun*), pres'āj or pre'sāj.
Presbyterian, prez-bĭ-te'rĭ-an, *not* pres-bĭ-te'rĭ-an.
presbytery, prez'bĭ-tĕr-ĭ, *not* pres-bit'er-ĭ.
prescience, pre'shĭ-ence, *not* pre'shence *nor* presh'ence. So **pre'sci-ent.**
presentation, prez-en-ta'shun, *not* prē-zen-ta'-shun.
presentiment, pre-sen'tĭ-ment, *not* pre-zen'ti-ment *nor* pre-zent'ment.
president, prez'ĭ-dent, *not* prez'ĭ-dunt.
prestige, pres'tēzh or pres'tij.
presumptuous, pre-zumt'u-us, *not* pre-zum'shus.
pretence, pre-tence', *not* pre'tence.
preterit, pret'er-it or pre'ter-it.
pretext, pre-tekst' or pre'tekst.
pretty, prit'ĭ, *not* prĕt'ĭ *nor* po͝ot'ĭ. So **pret'ti-ly.**
preventive, pre-ven'tiv, *not* pre-ven'ta-tiv.
primary, pri'ma-rĭ, *not* pri'mĕr-ĭ.
prism, prizm, *not* priz'um.

pristine, pris'tĭn, *not* pris'tīn.
prithee, pri*th*'e, *not* prith'e.
privacy, prī'va-sĭ, *not* prĭv'a-sĭ.
privily, prĭv'ĭ-lĭ, *not* prī'vĭ-lĭ.
probity, prob'ĭ-tĭ, *not* prō'bĭ-tĭ.
proceeds, pro'sēdz or pros'ēdz.
process, pros'es, *not* pro'ses.
procuress, pro-kūr'es, *not* prok'ū-res.
prodigy, prod'ĭ-jĭ, *not* proj'ĭ-dĭ.
produce, prod'ūce, *not* pro'dūce.
product, prod'ukt, *not* pro'dukt.
profile, pro'fēl or pro'fīl.
profuse, pro-fūs', *not* pro-fūz'.
progress (*noun*), prog'res, *not* pro'gres; (*verb*), pro-gres', *not* prog'res.
prohibition, pro-hĭ-bish'un, *not* pro-ī-bish'un.
prohibitory, pro-hib'ĭ-to-rĭ, *not* pro-hib'ĭ-ta-rĭ.
project (*noun*), proj'ekt, *not* pro'jekt.
projectile, pro-jek'tĭl, *not* pro-jek'tīl.
prolix, pro-liks', *not* pro'liks.
prolocutor, prol'o-ku-tur or pro-lok'u-tur.
prologue, prol'ŏg or pro'lŏg.
promenade, prom-ē-näd' or prom-e-nād'.
promissory, prom'is-so-rĭ, *not* pro-mis'so-rĭ.
promulgate, pro-mul'gāt, *not* prom'ul-gāt.
promulgation, prom-ul-ga'shun or pro-mul-ga'-shun.
promulgator, prom'ul-ga-tur or pro'mul-ga-tur.

pronunciation, pro-nun-sĭ-a′shun or pro-nun-shĭ-a′shun.

prophecy, prof′e-sĭ, *not* prof′e-sī.

prophesy (*verb*), prof′e-sī, *not* prof′e-sĭ.

propitiate, pro-pish′ĭ-āt, *not* pro-pish′āt.

prosaic, pro-za′ik, *not* pro-sa′ik.

prosody, pros′o-dĭ, *not* proz′o-dĭ.

prosperous, pros′per-us, *not* pros′prus.

Protean, pro′te-an or pro-te′an.

protégé, pro-tā-zha′, *not* prot′ā-zhā.

protest, prō′test or prŏt′est.

prothonotary, pro-thon′o-ta-rĭ, *not* pro-tho-no′-ta-rĭ.

protrude, pro-trōōd′, *not* pro-trūd′.

protrusive, pro-trōō′sĭv, *not* pro-trōō′ziv.

provocative, pro-vo′ka-tĭv or pro-vok′a-tiv.

provoke, pro-vōk′, *not* pur-vōk′.

provost, prŏv′ust or pro-vo′.

prowess, prow′es, *not* prō′es.

prude, prōōd, *not* prūd.

prudence, prōō′dence, *not* prū′dence.

prune, prōōn, *not* prūn.

Prussian, prush′an or prōō′shan.

prussic, prŭs′ik or prōōs′ik.

psalmist, säm′ist or sal′mist.

psalmody, sal′mo-dĭ, *not* säm′o-dĭ.

Psalms, sämz, *not* sămz.

psalter, sawl′ter or săl′ter.

puerile, pu′er-ĭl, *not* pu′er-īl.
puissance, pu′is-sance, or pu-is′sance.
puissant, pu′is-sant or pu-is′sant.
pumice, pu′mĭs or pum′is.
pumpkin, pump′kin, *but commonly pronounced* punk′in.
purport (*noun and verb*), pur′pōrt, *not* pur-pōrt′.
purulent, pu′ro͞o-lent, *not* pūr′yo͞o-lent.
Puseyism, pu′zĭ-izm, *not* pu′sĭ-izm.
pustule, pust′yo͞ol or pus′tūl, *not* pus′l.
put (*to place*), po͝ot, *not* pŭt.
pygmean, pig-me′an, *not* pig′me-an.
pyramidal, pĭ-ram′ĭ-dal, *not* pĭr′a-mid-al.
pyrites, pĭ-ri′tēz, *not* pĭr′ĭ-tēz.
Pythagorean, pĭ-thag-o-re′an or pĭth-a-go′re-an.
Pythoness, pĭth′o-nes, *not* pī-tho′nes.

Q.

quadrille, ka-dril′ or kwa-dril′, *not* kwod-ril′.
quadrupedal, kwad-ro͞o′pe-dal or kwad-ro͞o-pe′-dal.
quaggy, kwăg′ḡĭ, *not* kwog′ḡĭ.
quagmire, kwăg′mīr, *not* kwog′mīr.
quality, kwol′ĭ-tĭ, *not* kwol′ŭ-tĭ.
qualm, kwäm or kwawm.
quandary, kwon′da-rĭ or kwon-da′rĭ.
quantity, kwon′tĭ-tĭ, *not* kwon′tŭ-tĭ.

quarantine (*noun*), kwŏr′an-tēn; (*verb*), kwŏr-an-tēn′.
quarrel, kwŏr′el, *not* kwŏr′l.
quassia, kwosh′ĭ-a or kwăsh′ĭ-a, *not* kwosh′ĭ.
quinine, kwĭ-nīn′ or kwĭn′īn or kwī′nīn.
quoin, kwoin or koin.
quoit, kwoit, *not* kwāt.
quoth, kwōth or kwuth.

R.

rabbi, rab′bī or rab′bĭ.
radish, rad′ish, *not* red′ish.
raillery, răl′er-ĭ, *not* rāl′er-ĭ.
rapine, rap′ĭn, *not* rā′pēn.
raspberry, răz′bĕr-rĭ or răs′bĕr-rĭ, *not* rawz′ber-rĭ.
rather, ră*th*′er or rä*th*′er, *not* ru*th*′er.
ratio, rā′shĭ-o or rā′sho, *not* ră′sho.
ration, ra′shun, *not* rash′un.
rational, rash′un-al, *not* rā′shun-al. So **ra-tion-al′i-ty**, **ra′tion-al-ist**.
rationale, rash-ĭ-o-na′le or ra-shĭ-o-na′le.
realization, re-al-ĭ-za′shun, *not* re-al-īz-a′shun.
rebel, reb′el, *not* reb′l.
receptivity, res-ep-tiv′ĭ-tĭ, *not* re-sep-tiv′ĭ-tĭ.
recess, re-ses′, *not* re′ses.
Rechabite, re′kab-īt, *not* rek′ab-īt.

reciprocity, res´ĭ-pros´ĭ-tĭ, *not* re-sĭ-pros´ĭ-tĭ.
recitative, res-ĭ-ta-tēv´, *not* re-sīt´a-tĭv.
reclamation, rek-la-ma´shun, *not* re-kla-ma´shun.
recluse, re-klūs´, *not* re-klūz´.
recognizable, rek´og-nīz-a-bl or re-kog´nĭ-za-bl.
recognizance, re-kog´nĭ-zance or re-kon´ĭ-zance.
recognize, rek´og-nīz, *not* rek´o-nīz *nor* re-kog´-nīz.
recollect (*to call to mind*), rek-ol-lekt´, *not* re-kol-lekt´.
recondite, rek´on-dīt or re-kon´dīt.
reconnoissance, re-kon´nis-sänce, *not* re-kon-nois´sance.
reconnoitre, rek-on-noi´ter, *not* re-kon-noi´ter.
recourse, re-kōrce´, *not* re´kōrce.
recovery, re-kuv´er-ĭ, *not* re-kuv´rĭ.
recreant, rek´re-ant, *not* re´kre-ant.
recreate (*to give fresh life to*), rek´re-āt, *not* re´kre-āt. So **rec-re-a´tion**.
recruit, re-kro͞ot´, *not* re-krūt´.
rectitude, rek´tĭ-tūd, *not* rek´tĭ-to͞od.
recusant, re-ku´zant or rek´u-zant. So **recusancy**.
referable, rĕf´er-a-bl, *not* re-fer´a-bl.
reflex (*adj.*), re´fleks, *not* re-fleks´.
refuse, ref´yo͞os, *not* ref´yo͞oz.
refutable, re-fūt´a-bl, *not* ref´u-ta-bl.
regicide, rej´ĭ-sīd, *not* re´jĭ-sīd.
regress (*noun*), re´gres; (*verb*), re-gres´.

regular, reg′u-ler, *not* reg′ler.
relaxation, re-laks-a′shun or rel-aks-a′shun.
remediless, rem′e-dĭ-les or re-med′ĭ-les.
rendezvous, ren′de-vōō or ren′de-vōōz.
renew, re-nū′, *not* re-nōō′.
renunciation, re-nun-sĭ-a′shun or re-nun-shĭ-a′-shun.
reparable, rep′a-ra-bl, *not* re-pȧr′a-bl.
repartee, rep-ar-te′, *not* rep′ar-te.
reprimand (*verb*), rep′rĭ-mand or rep-rĭ-mand′; (*noun*), rep′rĭ-mand, *not* rep-rĭ-mand′.
reptile, rep′tĭl, *not* rep′tīl.
reputable, rep′u-ta-bl, *not* re-pūt′a-bl.
requiem, re′kwĭ-em or rek′wĭ-em.
research, re-serch′, *not* re′serch.
reservoir, rez-er-vwor′, *but commonly pronounced* rez′er-vwor.
residue, rez′ĭ-dū, *not* rez′ĭ-dōō.
resignation, rez-ig-na′shun, *not* res-ig-na′shun.
resin, rez′in, *not* rez′n.
resonance, rez′o-nance, *not* res′o-nance.
resource, re-sōrce′, *not* re′sōrce.
respirable, re-spīr′a-bl, *not* res′pĭ-ra-bl.
respite (*noun and verb*), res′pĭt, *not* res′pīt.
respited, res′pit-ed, *not* re-spīt′ed.
restorative, re-stōr′a-tĭv, *not* res-tŏr′a-tĭv.
retail (*verb*), re-tāl′, *not* re′tāl; (*noun*), re′tāl, *not* re-tāl′.

retailer, re-tāl′er or re′tāl-er.
retardation, re-tar-da′shun, or ret-ar-da′shun.
retch, rĕch or rēch.
retributive, re-trib′u-tiv, *not* ret′rĭ-bu-tiv *nor* ret-rĭ-bu′tiv.
retroact, re-tro-akt′ or ret-ro-akt′. So **retro-ac′tive,** &c.
retrocede, re′tro-sēd or ret′ro-sēd. So **retro-ces′sion.**
retrograde, re′tro-grād or ret′ro-grăd. So **retro-gres′sion.**
retrospect, re′tro-spekt or ret′ro-spekt. So **re-trospec′tion,** &c.
retrovert, re′tro-vert or ret′ro-vert. So **retro-ver′sion.**
reveille, re-vāl′yā or re-vāl′.
revelry, rev′el-rĭ, *not* rev′l-rĭ.
revenue, rev′e-nū; re-ven′yōō *is obsolete.*
reverie, rev-er-e′ or rev′er-e.
revery, rev′er-ĭ, *not* rev-er-e′.
revocable, rev′o-ka-bl, *not* re-vo′ka-bl.
revolt, re-vōlt′ or re-vŏlt′. So **revolt′ing.**
Reynard, ra′nard or ren′ard.
rhomb, rŏmb, *not* rŏm.
rhubarb, rōō′barb, *not* rōō′bub.
rhythm, rithm or ri*th*m.
rhythmic, rith′mik or ri*th*′mik.
rhythmical, rith′mĭ-kal or ri*th*′mĭ-kal.

ribald, rib′ăld, *not* ri′bald *nor* rib′awld. So **rib′-ald-ry.**

rid, rid, *not* red.

ridicule, rid′i-kūl, *not* red′i-kūl.

ridiculous, rĭ-dik′u-lus, *not* rĭ-dik′lus.

rind, rīnd, *not* rīn.

rinse, rĭnse, *not* rĕnse.

rise (*noun*), rīs or rīz.

risk, risk, *not* resk.

robust, ro-bust′, *not* ro′bust.

roil, roil, *not* rīl.

romance, ro-mance′, *not* ro′mance.

roof, rōōf, *not* rŏŏf *nor* rŭf.

rook, rŏŏk, *not* rōōk. So **rook′er-y.**

room, rōōm, *not* rŏŏm.

roost, rōōst, *not* rŏŏst.

root, rōōt, *not* rŏŏt.

roseate, ro′ze-āt, *not* ro′zhe-āt.

route, rōōt or rowt.

routine, rōō-tēn′, *not* rōō′tēn.

ruby, rōō′bĭ, *not* rū′bĭ.

rude, rōōd, *not* rūd.

rudiment, rōō′dĭ-ment, *not* rū′dĭ-ment.

rue, rōō, *not* rū.

ruffian, ruf′yan or ruf′ĭ-an, *not* ruf′in.

ruin, rōō′in, *not* rū′in. So **ru′in-ous.**

rule, rōōl, *not* rūl.

rumor, rōō′mur, *not* rū′mur.

rural, ro͞o'ral, *not* rū'ral.
Russian, rush'an or ro͞o'shan.
ruthless, ro͞oth'les, *not* rūth'les.

S.

saccharine, sak'a-rĭn or sak'a-rīn.
sacerdotal, sas-er-do'tal, *not* sā-ser-do'tal.
sacrament, sak'ra-ment, *not* sā'kra-ment.
sacrifice (*noun*), sak'rĭ-fīz or sak'rĭ-fīs, *not* sa'krĭ-fīz.
sacrifice (*verb*), sak'rĭ-fīz, *not* sa'krĭ-fīz.
sacrilege, sak'rĭ-lĕj, *not* sa'krĭ-lĭj.
sacrilegious, sak-rĭ-le'jus, *not* sak-rĭ-lĭj'us.
sacristan, sak'ris-tan, *not* sa-kris'tan. So **sac'-ris-ty**.
saffron, saf'run; saf'urn *is obsolete.*
sagacious, sa-ga'shus, *not* sa-gash'us.
said, sed, *not* sād.
salary, sal'a-rĭ, *not* sal'rĭ.
Salic, sal'ik, *not* sa'lik.
salient, sa'lĭ-ent, *not* sal'ĭ-ent.
saline, sa-līn' or sa'līn, *not* sa'lēn.
saliva, sa-lī'va, *not* sal'i-va.
salmon, săm'un, *not* säm'un.
salute, sa-lūt', *not* sa-lo͞ot'.
salve, säv, *not* săv.
salver (*a plate*), săl'ver, *not* sä'ver.

Samaritan, sa-măr'ĭ-tan, *not* sa-mā'rĭ-tan.
samphire, sam'fur or sam'fīr.
sandwich, sand'wich or sand'wij.
sanguine, sang'gwĭn, *not* san'gwĭn. So **san'-guin-a-ry, san-guin'e-ous.**
sapience, sa'pĭ-ence, *not* săp'ĭ-ence. So **sa'pi-ent.**
sapphire, saf'fur or saf'fīr.
sarcenet, sars'net, *not* sar'se-net.
sardine (*a fish*), sar'dēn or sar'dĭn.
sardonyx, sar'do-niks, *not* sar-do'niks.
sarsaparilla, sar-sa-pa-ril'la, *not* sas-a-pa-ril'la.
sat, sat, *not* sot.
satiate, sa'shĭ-āt, *not* sa'shāt.
satin, sat'in, *not* sat'n.
satire, sat'īr or sat'er. In England sat'er is preferred, in the United States sat'īr.
satrap, sa'trap or sat'rap.
saturnine, sat'ur-nīn, *not* sa'tur-nīn *nor* sat'ur-nĭn.
satyr, sa'ter or sat'er.
saucy, saw'sĭ, *not* săs'ĭ *nor* sä'sĭ.
saunter, sän'ter or sawn'ter.
sausage, saw'sej, *not* săs'ej.
scabious, ska'bĭ-us, *not* skab'ĭ-us.
scald (*to burn with fluid*), skawld, *not* skŏld.
scald (*a bard*), skăld or skawld.
scalene, ska-lēn', *not* ska'lēn.
scallop, skol'lup, *not* skăl'lup.
scaramouch, skăr'a-mowch, *not* skăr'a-mōōch.

scarce, skȧrce, *not* skärce *nor* skurce. So **scarce′ly**.
scared, skȧrd, *not* skȧrt.
scathed, skătht or skā*th*d.
scathing, skăth′ing or skā*th*′ing.
scenic, sen′ik or sēn′ik.
sceptic, skep′tik, *not* sep′tik.
schedule, sked′yo͞ol or sed′yo͞ol or shed′yo͞ol.
schism, sizm, *not* siz′um.
schismatic (*noun*), siz′ma-tik or siz-mat′ik; (*adj.*), siz-mat′ik.
schooner, sko͞on′er, *not* sko͝on′er.
scorbutic, skor-bu′tik, *not* skor-but′ik.
scoundrel, skown′drel, *not* skown′dl.
screw, skro͞o, *not* skrū.
scrivener, skrĭv′ner, *not* skrīv′ner.
scrofula, skrŏf′u-la, *not* skrawf′u-la.
scrupulous, skro͞o′pu-lus, *not* skro͞op′lus.
scrutinize, skro͞o′tĭ-nīz, *not* skrū′ti-nīz.
seamstress, sēm′stres or sĕm′stres.
seckel (*a pear*), sek′l, *not* sik′l.
seclude, se-klūd′, *not* se-klo͞od′.
secretary, sek′re-ta-rĭ, *not* sek′ŭ-ta-rĭ.
secretory, se-krēt′o-rĭ or se′kre-to-rĭ.
sedative, sed′a-tiv, *not* se-da′tiv.
seine, sēn, *not* sān.
senile, se′nīl, *not* se′nĭl.
senna, sen′na, *not* sē′na *nor* sē′nĭ.

sentient, sen′shĭ-ent, *not* sen′shent.
sentiment, sen′tĭ-ment, *not* sen′tĭ-munt.
separatist, sep′a-ra-tist, *not* sep-a-ra′tist.
sepulture, sep′ul-tūr, *not* se-pul′tūr.
sequel, se′kwel, *not* se′kwil.
sequestration, sek-wes-tra′shun, *not* se′kwes-tra′shun.
series, se′rĭ-ēz or se′rēz.
sergeant, sar′jant or ser′jant.
servile, ser′vĭl, *not* ser′vīl.
seventy, sev′en-tĭ, *not* sev′un-tĭ.
several, sev′er-al, *not* sev′rul.
sew, so, *not* sū.
sewer (*a drain*), sōōr or su′er.
shall, shăl, *not* sh'l.
sha' n't (*shall not*), shänt, *not* shănt.
sheath (*noun*), shēth; **sheaths** (*pl.*), shē*thz*, *not* shēths.
shekel, shek′l, *not* she′kl.
shew, shō, *not* shū.
shire, shēr or shīr.
shone, shŏn or shōn.
short-lived, short′-līvd, *not* short′-lĭvd.
shrew, shrōō, *not* shrū *nor* srōō.
shrewd, shrōōd, *not* shrūd *nor* srōōd.
shriek, shrēk, *not* srēk.
shrill, shril, *not* sril.
shrine, shrīn, *not* srīn.

shrub, shrub, *not* srub.
shrug, shrug, *not* srug.
shut, shut, *not* shet.
sibyl, sib′il, *not* sī′bil.
sibylline, sib′il-līn or sib′il-lĭn.
simile, sĭm′ĭ-lē, *not* sim′īl.
simony, sim′o-nĭ, *not* sī′mo-nĭ.
simultaneous, si-mul-ta′ne-us or sim-ul-ta′ne-us.
since, since, *not* sence.
sinecure, si′ne-kūr, *not* sin′e-kūr.
sinew, sin′ū, *not* sin′o͞o.
singular, sing′gū-lar, *not* sing′glar.
siren, si′ren, *not* sĭr′en.
sirrah, sĭr′ra or săr′ra.
sirup, sĭr′up, *colloquially*, sur′rup.
sit, sit, *not* set.
sixth, sĭksth, *not* sĭkst.
slabber, slăb′ber, *colloquially*, slob′ber.
sleek, slēk, *not* slik.
slept, slept, *not* slep.
sliver, sli′ver or sliv′er.
sloth, slōth, *not* slŏth.
slough (*a scab*), sluf, *not* slăoo.
slough (*a mire-hole*), slow, *not* sluf.
sloven, sluv′en or sluv′n, *not* slov′n.
smallpox, smawl′poks or smawl-poks′.
smutch, smuch, *not* smo͞och.
snout, snowt, *not* sno͞ot.

sociable, so'shĭ-a-bl or so'sha-bl.
sociality, so-shĭ-al'ĭ-tĭ, *not* so-shăl'ĭ-tĭ.
sofa, so'fa, *not* so'fĭ.
soft,[4] soft, *not* sawft.
soften,[4] sof'n, *not* sof'ten *nor* sawf'ten.
softly,[4] soft'lĭ, *not* sof'lĭ *nor* sawft'lĭ.
soiree, swä-rā' or swaw-rā'.
sojourn (*noun and verb*), so'jurn, *not* so-jurn'.
sol (*in music*), sōl or sŏl.
solder, sol'der or saw'der.
solecism, sol'e-sĭzm, *not* so'le-sĭzm.
solemn, sol'em, *not* sol'um.
solstice, sŏl'stis, *not* sōl'stis *nor* sol'stīs.
solution, so-lū'shun, *not* so-lōō'zhun.
sombre, sōm'ber or sŏm'ber. So **som'brous.**
something, sum'thing, *not* sun'thin.
somewhat, sum'hwot, *not* sum'wot.
somewhere, sum'hwâr, *not* sum'hwär *nor* sum'-hwârz.
sonnet, sŏn'net, *not* sun'net.
sonorous, so-no'rus, *not* son'o-rus.
soot, sŏŏt or sōōt, *not* sŭt. So **soot'y**.
soothsayer, sōōth'sā-er, *not* sōō*th*'sā-er.
soporific, sop-o-rif'ik, *not* sō-po-rif'ik.
sorry, sŏr'rĭ, *not* saw'rĭ.
sortie, sor'te or sor-te'.
sough, suf, *not* sow. So **sough'ing.**
souse (*verb*), sows, *not* sowz.

southerly, su*th*'er-lĭ or sow*th*'er-lĭ. So **south'ern.**
southward, sowth'ward or su*th*'urd.
sovereign, suv'er-in or sŏv'er-in.
spaniel, span'yel, *not* span'el.
spasm, spazm, *not* spaz'um.
species, spe'shēz or spe'shĕz.
specious, spe'shus, *not* spesh'us.
spectacles, spek'ta-klz, *not* spet'a-klz.
spermaceti, sperm-a-se'tĭ, *not* sperm-a-sit'ī *nor* spar-ma-sit'ī.
spheroid, sphe'roid, *not* sphĕr'oid.
spinach, spin'āj, *not* spin'ātsh.
spinet, spin'et or spĭ-net'.
spiracle, spĭr'a-kl or spi'ra-kl.
spirit, spĭr'it, *not* spĕr'it *nor* spe'rit.
splenetic, splen'e-tik, *not* sple-net'ik.
spoon, spo͞on, *not* spo͝on.
spouse, spowz, *not* spows.
squalid, skwŏl'id, *not* skwăl'id *nor* skwawl'id.
squalor, skwā'lawr, *not* skwŏl'er.
squirrel, skwŭr'el or skwĭr'el or skwĕr'el.
stalwart, stawl'wart, *not* stăl'wart.
stamp, stămp, *not* stŏmp.
stanch, stänch, *not* stănch *nor* stawnch.
stand, stand, *not* stan.
starboard, star'bōrd, *colloquially*, starb'urd.
statics, stăt'iks, *not* stā'tiks.
statu quo [L.], stā'tū kwo, *not* stat'yo͞o kwo.

staves, stāves or stävz.
steady, stĕd'ĭ, *not* stĭd'ĭ.
steelyard, stēl'yard, *colloquially*, stĭl'yard.
stereoscope, stē're-o-skōp or stĕr'e-o-skōp.
stereotype, stē're-o-tīp or stĕr'e-o-tīp.
steward, stū'ard, *not* stōō'ard.
stint, stĭnt, *not* stĕnt.
stirrup, stur'up or stĕr'up.
stolid, stol'id, *not* sto'lid.
stomacher, stum'a-cher, *not* stum'a-ker.
stomachic, sto-mak'ik, *not* sto-mat'ik.
stone, stōn, *not* stun.
stony, sto'nĭ, *not* stun'ĭ.
storm, storm, *not* stawm.
strata, strā'ta, *not* strä'ta. So **stra'tum.**
strategic, stra-te'jik or stra-tej'ik.
strength, strength, *not* strenth.
strew, strōō or strō.
strychnine, strik'nīn, *not* strik'nĭn.
student, stū'dent, *not* stōō'dent *nor* stūd'nt.
stupendous, stū-pen'dus, *not* stu-pend'yōō-us *nor* stu-pen'jus.
stupid, stū'pid, *not* stōō'pid.
suasory, swa'so-rĭ, *not* swa'zo-rĭ.
suavity, swav'ĭ-tĭ, *not* su-av'ĭ-tĭ.
subaltern, sub'ăl-tern or sub-awl'tern.
subdue, sub-dū', *not* sub-dōō'.
subjected, sub-jekt'ed, *not* sub'jekt-ed.

sublunary, sub′lu-na-rĭ, *not* sub-lu′na-rĭ.
subpœna, sub-pe′na, *not* sup-pe′na.
subsidence, sub-sīd′ence, *not* sub′si-dence.
substantiate, sub-stan′shĭ-āt, *not* sub-stan′shāt.
substantively, sub′stan-tiv-lĭ, *not* sub-stan′tiv-lĭ.
subtile (*thin or rare*), sub′tĭl, *not* sub′tīl.
subtle (*sly*), sut′l, *not* sub′tl.
succumb, suk-kumb′, *not* suk-kum′.
such, such, *not* sech *nor* sich.
sudden, sud′dĕn, *not* sud′n *nor* sud′ding. So **sud′den-ly**.
suffice, suf-fīz,′ *not* suf-fīs′.
suggest, sug-jest′ or sud-jest′.
suicidal, su′ĭ-sīd-al, *not* su-ĭ-sīd′al.
suite, swēt, *not* sūt *nor* sōōt.
sulphuric, sul-fu′rik, *not* sul′fur-ik.
sultana, sul-tā′na or sul-tä′na.
sumach, sū′mak or shōō′mak.
summary, sum′ma-rĭ, *not* sum′mĕr-ĭ.
summoned, sum′mund, *not* sum′munzd.
supererogatory, su-per-ĕr′o-ga-to-rĭ or su-per-e-rog′a-to-rĭ.
superficies, su-per-fĭsh′ĭ-ēz or su-per-fish′ēz.
supple, sup′l, *not* sōō′pl.
suppose, sup-pōz′, *not* spōz.
surnamed, sur-nāmd′, *not* sur′nāmd.
surprise, sur-prīz′, *not* sup-prīz′.
surtout, sur-tōōt′, *not* sur′tōōt.

surveillance, sur-văl'yănce, *not* sōōr-văl-yănce'.
survey (*noun*), sur'vā or sur-vā'; (*verb*), sur-vā'.
swarthy, swawr'thĭ, *not* swawr'*th*ĭ.
swath, swawth or swŏth.
swept, swept, *not* swep.
swiftly, swift'lĭ, *not* swif'lĭ.
swingel, swin'jel or swing'gl.
sword, sōrd, *not* swōrd.
synod, sin'od, *not* sī'nod.
syrup, sĭr'up, *colloquially*, sŭr-up.

T.

tabernacle, tab'er-na-kl or tab'er-năk-l.
tableau, tab-lo' or tab'lo.
talc, tălk, *not* tawk.
talcose, tal-kōs', *not* tăl'kōs *nor* tăl-kōz'.
talisman, tăl'iz-man or tăl'is-man.
tapestry, tap'es-trĭ, *not* tāps'trĭ.
tapis, tā'pis or tä-pe'.
tarpaulin, tar-pawl'in, *not* tar-po'lin.
Tartarean, tar-ta're-an, *not* tar-ta-re'an.
tartaric, tär-tăr'ik, *not* tär-tär'ik.
tassel, tăs'sĕl or tos'l, *not* taw'sel.
tatterdemalion, tat-ter-de-măl'yun, *not* tat-ter-de-māl'yun.
taunt, tänt or tawnt.
tavern, tăv'ern, *not* tär'vern.

teat, tēt, *not* tit.
tedious, te′dĭ-us or tēd′yus.
telegraphist, te-leg′ra-fist, *not* tel′e-graf-ist. So **te-leg′ra-phy.**
temperament, tem′per-a-ment, *not* tem′per-munt.
temperature, tem′per-ȧ-tūr, *not* tem′per-to͞or.
tenable, ten′a-bl, *not* te′na-bl.
tenacious, te-na′shus, *not* te-nash′us.
tenet, ten′et, *not* te′net.
tenure, tĕn′yo͞or, *not* tēn′yo͞or.
tepid, tep′id, *not* te′pid.
tepor, te′por or tep′or.
tergiversation, ter-jĭ-ver-sa′shun, *not* ter-ḡĭ-ver-sa′shun.
terrapin, tĕr′ra-pin, *not* tur′ra-pin.
thanksgiving, thanks′ḡiv-ing, *not* thanks-ḡiv′ing.
therefore, *th*er′fōr or *th*ȧr′fōr.
thereof, *th*ȧr′ŏf or *th*ȧr′ŏv′.
therewith, *th*ȧr-with′ or *th*ȧr-wi*th*′.
thither, *thith*′er, *not* thi*th*′er.
thoroughly, thur′o-lĭ, *not* thur′ŭ-lĭ.
thousand, thow′zand, *not* thow′zan.
thraldom, thrawl′dum, *not* thrŏl′dum.
three-legged, thrē-legd′, *not* thrē-leg′ḡed.
threepence, thrē′pence, *colloquially*, thrip′ence. So **threepen-ny.**
threshold, thresh′ōld or thresh′hōld.
threw, thro͞o, *not* thrū.

thyme, tīm, *not* thīm.
tiara, tĭ-ā'ra, *not* tĭ-ä'ra.
ticklish, tick'lish, *not* tick'l-ish.
tierce, tērce or turce.
tiny, tī'nĭ, *not* tē'nĭ *nor* tĭn'ĭ.
tirade, tĭ-rād' or tĭ-räd', *not* tī'rād.
to, tōō, *not* tŭ.
tongs,[4] tongz, *not* tawngz.
tomato, to-mā'to or to-mä'to.
tonsure, ton'shur, *not* ton'sōōr.
toothache, tōōth'āk, *not* teeth'āk.
toothed, tōōtht, *not* tōō*th*d.
topographical, top-o-graf'ik-al, *not* tō-po-graf'-ik-al. So **top-o-graph'ic.**
tortoise, tor'tiz or tor'tis, *not* tor'tois.
tossing,[4] tos'ing, *not* tost'ing.
tottering, tot'ter-ing, *not* tot'tring.
toucan, tōō'kan or tow'kan.
tour, tōōr, *not* towr. So **tour'ist.**
tournament, tōōr'na-ment or tur'na-ment.
tourney, tōōr'nĭ or tur'nĭ.
toward, tō'urd, *not* tō-wawrd'.
trachea, tra'ke-a or tra-ke'a.
tragacanth, trag'a-kanth, *not* traj'a-kanth.
tranquil, trang'kwil, *not* tran'kwil.
transact, trans-akt', *not* tranz-akt'.
transferable, trans-fĕr'a-bl, *not* trans-fer'a-bl.
transferrence, trans-fĕr'rence, *not* trans-fer'rence.

transferrible, trans-fĕr′rĭ-bl, *not* trans-fer′rĭ-bl.
transition, tran-sizh′un, *not* trans-ish′un.
transmigrate, trans′mĭ-grāt, *not* trans-mī′grāt.
transparent, trans-pȧr′ent, *not* trans-pā′rent.
trapezium, tra-pe′zĭ-um or tra-pe′zhĭ-um.
trapezoid, trap′e-zoid or trap-e-zoid′.
travel, trav′el, *not* trav′l.
traveller, trav′el-ler, *not* trav′ler.
treatise, trēt′iz or trēt′is.
treble, treb′l, *not* trib′l *nor* thrib′l.
tremendous, tre-men′dus, *not* tre-mend′yōō-us *nor* tre-men′jus.
tremor, tre′mur or trem′ur.
tribunal, trī-bu′nal, *not* trĭ-bu′nal.
tribune, trib′ūn, *not* trī′būn.
trilobite, tri′lo-bīt *not* tril′o-bīt.
trio, trī′o or trē′o.
tripartite, trip′ar-tīt *not* trī-par′tīt.
triphthong,[4] trip′thong or trif′thong.
trisyllable, trĭ-sil′la-bl, or tris′il-la-bl.
triune, tri′ūn, *not* tri′ōōn.
trivial, triv′ĭ-al, *not* triv′yal.
troche, tro′kē, *not* trōk *nor* tro′chē.
troll (*a fabled dwarf*), trōl l, *not* trŏll.
trombone, trom′bōn (*Italian* trom-bo′nā), *not* trom-bōn′.
trophy, tro′fĭ, *not* trŏf′ĭ.
troth,[4] troth, *not* trōth.

trough,[4] trof, *not* trawf *nor* trawth.
trow, trō, *not* trow.
truculent, trōō'ku-lent, *not* trŭk'u-lent.
true, trōō, *not* trū.
truffle, trōō'fl, *not* trŭf'l.
truths, trōōths, *not* trōō*thz.*
tryst, trĭst, *not* trīst. So **tryst'ing-place.**
tube, tūb, *not* tōōb.
tuberose, tūb'rōz or tū'ber-ōs.
Tuesday, tūz'dĭ, *not* tōōz'dĭ.
tulip, tū'lip, *not* tōō'lip.
tumor, tū'mur, *not* tōō'mur.
tumult, tū'mult, *not* tōō'mult.
tune, tūn, *not* tōōn.
turbine, tur'bĭn, *not* tur'bīn.
turquoise, tur-koiz' or tur-kēz'.
twopence, tōō'pence, *colloquially,* tup'ence.
typhus, ti'fus, *not* ti'pus.
typographical, tĭp-o-graf'ik-al or ti-po-graf'ik-al. So **typog'ra-phy, typog'ra-pher.**
tyrannic, tī-ran'nik, *not* tĭ-ran'nik.

U.

ultimatum, ul-tĭ-mā'tum, *not* ul-tĭ-mä'tum.
umbrageous, um-bra'jus or um-bra'je-us.
umbrella, um-brel'la, *not* um-brĭl'la *nor* um-ber-el'a *nor* um-ber-el'.

uncouth, un-kōōth′, *not* un-kōō*th*′.
unctuous, unkt′yōō-us, *not* unk′shus.
underneath, un-der-nē*th*′, *not* un-der-nēth′.
undersigned, un-der-sīnd′, *not* un′der-sīnd.
unerring, un-ĕr′ring or un-er′ring.
unguent, ung′gwent, *not* un′gwent.
unguentum, ung-gwen′tum, *not* an-gwin′tum.
unison, yōō′nĭ-sun, *not* yōō′nĭ-zun.
unscathed, un-skătht′ or un-skă*th*d′.
Uranus, u′ra-nus, *not* u-ra′nus.
ureter, u′re-ter or u-re′ter.
usage, yōō′zij, *not* yōō′sij.
usufruct, u′zu-frukt, *not* u′su-frukt.
usurious, yōō-zhōō′rĭ-us or yōō-zŭ′rĭ-us.
usurp, u-zurp′, *not* u-surp′. So **u-sur-pa′tion.**
uterine, u′ter-īn or u′ter-īn.
uxorious, ugz-o′rĭ-us, *not* uks-o′rĭ-us.

V.

vaccinate, vak′sĭ-nāt, *not* vas′sĭ-nāt. So **vac-ci-na′tion.**
vaccine, vak′sīn or vak′sĭn.
vagary, va-ga′rĭ, *not* vă′ga-rĭ.
valet, val′et or val′ā.
valise, va-lēs′ or va-lēz′.
valuable, val′u-a-bl, *not* val′yŭ-bl.
variegated, va′rĭ-e-gāt-ed, *not* va-rĭ′e-gāt′ed.

varioloid, vā'rĭ-o-loid, *not* văr'ĭ-o-loid *nor* văr'ĭ-loid.
vase, vās or vāz.
vaticinal, va-tis'ĭ-nal, *not* vat-ĭ-si'nal.
vaunt, vawnt or vänt.
vehement, ve'he-ment, *not* ve-he'ment. So **ve'-he-mence.**
velvet, vel'vet, *not* vel'vit.
vendue, ven-dū', *not* van-dōō'.
venial, ve'nĭ-al, *not* vēn'yal.
venison, ven'ĭ-zn or ven'zn.
verbose, ver-bōs', *not* ver-bōz'.
verdigris, ver'dĭ-grēs, *not* ver'dĭ-grĭs.
vermicelli, ver-mĭ-chel'lĭ or ver-mĭ-sel'lĭ.
vertigo, ver'tĭ-go, *pedantically,* ver-tī'go or ver-te'go.
vesicatory, ves'i-ka-to-rĭ or ve-sik'a-to-rĭ.
vessel, ves'sel, *not* ves'l.
veterinary, vet'er-e-na-rĭ, *not* vet'rĭ-nur-ĭ.
vibratory, vi'bra-to-rĭ, *not* vib'ra-to-rĭ.
vicar, vik'ar, *not* vi'kar.
vicinity, vĭ-sin'i-tĭ, *not* vī-sin'i-tĭ.
victory, vik'to-rĭ, *not* vik'trĭ.
vignette, vin-yet', *not* vin-et'.
vigorous, vig'o-rus, *not* vig'rus.
villain, vil'lin, *not* vil'un.
vindicative, vin'dĭ-ka-tiv, *not* vin-dik'a-tiv. So **vin'di-ca-to-ry.**

vineyard, vin'yard, *not* vīn'yard.
violent, vi'o-lent, *not* voi'lent. So **vi'o-lence.**
violet, vi'o-let, *not* voi'let.
violoncello, ve-o-lon-chel'lo or ve-o-lon-sel'lo.
virago, vĭ-rä'go or vī-rā'go, *not* vĭ-rä'go.
virile, vī'rĭl or vĭr'ĭl. So **viril'ity.**
viscount, vī'kownt, *not* vis'kownt.
visor, viz'ur, *not* vī'zur.
vitiate, vish'ĭ-āt, *not* vish'āt.
vitriol, vit'rĭ-ul, *not* vit'rul.
vituperate, vĭ-tu'per-āt or vī-tu'per-āt.
vivacious, vĭ-va'shus or vī-va'shus. So **vivac'-ity.**
vizier, vĭz'yer or vĭ-zēr', *not* vīz'yer.
vocable, vo'ka-bl, *not* vok'a-bl.
vocule, vōk'ūl or vŏk'ūl.
volatile, vol'a-tĭl, *not* vol'a-tīl.
volume, vol'yum or vol'yo͞om.
volute, vo-lūt', *not* vol'ūt.
voyage, voi'ej, *colloquially,* voij.
vulpine, vul'pĭn, *not* vul'pīn.

W.

wainscot, wān'skot, *colloquially,* wen'skut.
waistcoat, wāst'kōt, *colloquially,* wes'kut.
walnut, wawl'nut or wŏl'nut.
walrus, wawl'rus or wŏl'rus.

wampum, wawm′pum or wŏm′pum.
wan, wŏn, *not* wăn.
wandering, wŏn′der-ing, *not* wŏn′dring.
want, wawnt or wŏnt.
warrant, wŏr′rant, *not* wawr′ant.
warrior, wawr′yur or wŏr′ri-ur.
was, wŏz, *not* wuz.
wassail, wos′sil, *not* wăs′sāl.
water, waw′ter, *not* wot′er.
weapon, wep′un or wep′n.
weary, wē′rĭ or wēr′ĭ.
weasand, wē′zand or wē′znd.
well, wel, *not* wăl.
wept, wept, *not* wep.
were, wer, *not* wăur.
westward, west′ward, *not* west′urd.
wharf, hworf, *not* worf.
what, hwot, *not* wot.
where, hwȧr, *not* wăur.
wherefore, hwȧr′fōr, *not* hwer′fōr.
whereof, hwȧr-of′ or hwȧr-ov′.
wherewith, hwȧr-with′ or hwar-wi*th*′.
whether, hwe*th*′er, *not* we*th*′er.
which, hwich, *not* wich.
while, hwīl, *not* wīl.
whinny, hwin′nĭ, *not* win′nĭ.
whisk, hwisk, *not* wisk.
whiskey, hwisk′ĭ, *not* wis′kĭ.

whistle, hwis'l, *not* hwis'tl *nor* wis'l.
white, hwīt, *not* wīt.
whither, hwi*th*'er, *not* wi*th*'er.
whole, hōl, *not* hŭl. So **whole'sale, whole'-some.**
whooping-cough, hōōp'ing-kof, *not* hŏŏp'ing-kof.
whorl, hworl or hwurl.
whortleberry, hwur'tl-bĕr-rĭ, *not* hwor'tl-bĕr-rĭ. *Commonly spelled and pronounced* **huck'le-ber-ry,** huk'l-bĕr-rĭ.
why, hwī, *not* wī.
wife's (*possessive case*), wīfs, *not* wīvz.
wigwam, wig'wawm or wig'wom.
window, win'do, *not* win'der.
windpipe, wĭnd'pīp or wīnd'pīp.
windrow, wĭn'rō or wĭnd'rō.
windward, wĭnd'ward, *not* wĭnd'urd.
wiseacre, wīz'a-ker, *not* wīz-a'ker.
with, wi*th*, *not* with. So **withdraw', with-hold',** &c.
withe, wĭth, *not* wĭ*th*.
won't, wōnt, *not* wŭnt.
worse, wurs, *not* wus.
worship, wur'ship, *not* wush'ip.
worst, wurst, *not* wust.
worsted, wōōrs'ted or wŏŏs'ted.
worth, wurth, *not* wuth.

worthy, wur'*th*ĭ, *not* wu*th*'ĭ.
wound (*noun and verb*), wōōnd or wownd.
wrath, räth or rawth. So **wrath'ful**.
wreath (*noun*), rēth, *not* rē*th*; **wreaths** (*n. pl.*), rē*th*z, *not* rēths.
wrestle, res'l, *not* res'tl *nor* ras'l.
wristband, rist'band, *colloquially*, riz'band.
wrong,[4] rong, *not* rawng.
wroth,[4] rawth or rŏth.

X.

xylographic, zī-lo-graf'ik, *not* zĭl-o-graf'ik. So **xy-log'ra-pher**, **xy'lo-graph**.
xiphoid, zif'oid, *not* zī'foid.

Y.

yacht, yot, *not* yat.
yea, yā; yē *is obsolete.*
yellow, yel'lo, *not* yel'ler *nor* yăl'lo.
yes, yĕs, *not* yĭs *nor* yăas *nor* yĕ.
yesterday, yes'ter-dā, *not* yis'ter-dā.
yet, yĕt, *not* yĭt.
yolk, yōk or yōlk.
you,[3] yōō, *not* yĭoo *nor* yŭ.
yonder, yon'der, *not* yen'der *nor* yun'der.
yourself, yōōr-self', *not* yĕr-self'.
youths, yōōths, *not* yōō*th*z.

Z.

zealot, zĕl′ut, *not* zēl′ut.
zenith, ze′nith, *not* zen′ith.
zoology, zo-ol′o-jĭ, *not* zōō-ol′o-jĭ *nor* zōō′lo-jĭ.
zoological, zo-o-loj′ĭ-kal, *not* zōō-o-loj′ĭ-kal.
zouave, zŏŏ-äv′ or zwäv, *not* zōō-ăv′.

PRONOUNCING HANDBOOK.

RECOMMENDATIONS.

From ABNER J. PHIPPS, *General Agent of the Board of Education, Mass.*

Mispronunciation even of many common words, in every-day use, is so frequent that I have often made the subject a prominent one in my talks to teachers at our Institutes, and in my visits to the Schools throughout the State, with the hope of thus doing something to correct the evil. As this Pronouncing Handbook has in view a similar object, I very cordially commend it to all, and especially to the many teachers who have expressed to me a wish for the publication of such a book.

From WILLIAM A. WHEELER, *Editor of Webster's Series of Dictionaries.*

The Handbook really meets a public want which has never been adequately met before. I have a pretty extensive acquaintance with other works of a similar scope, and I am quite safe in saying that they are all too meagre, or too full of crotchets, or else that they carry with them too little weight of editorial authority to have much value. Your manual is of a different stamp and merits hearty commendation . . . If all would buy it who need the information it contains, it would, perhaps, be the most widely circulated book in the language.

From PROF. W. D. WHITNEY, *of Yale College.*

I should think it would attract general attention, and fill the needs of many.

From GEO. A. WALTON, *Agent of the State Board of Education, Mass.*

If this little book can be put into the hands of all persons ambitious to pronounce the language correctly, it will prove the best contribution made within my knowledge to accurate scholarship in this very important matter of pronunciation. It should be not only the Handbook, but the pocket-book, for all students; for everybody. It is "neat as a pin."

PRONOUNCING HANDBOOK.

COMMENDATIONS FROM THE PRESS.

This book can be carried in a gentleman's vest pocket or tucked into a lady's belt, and we wish several hundred thousand copies might be so disposed of with a view to daily consultation. — *The Congregationalist.*

The editors have performed their work with judgment and good taste, and it will be found a very desirable assistant in an essential accomplishment. — *The Christian Intelligencer.*

The correct pronunciation is indicated by an admirably simple system of phonetic spelling. —*The Harvard Advocate.*

A careful examination satisfies us, that it is of real value. —*The Mercury.*

A little book of great value. — *Portland Advertiser.*

We commend it as a trustworthy guide which should have a place on the study table. — *The Christian Era.*

It might be profitably used in schools as well as by private learners. — *Albany Evening Times.*

In the education of youth, we think especial attention should be given to this collection of words. — *The Pilot.*

It should find its way into our schools, and be in daily use in our homes. — *Worcester Palladium.*

We venture the prediction that ninety-nine persons out of every hundred in any average community, who should look this list through, would be greatly surprised to find how many words they are mispronouncing every day. — *Vermont Phœnix.*

An exceedingly handy and serviceable little book. — *The Chicago Standard.*

After a pretty careful examination, we cordially commend the very thorough and accurate manner in which the work has been done. —*Hearth and Home.*

www.ingramcontent.com/pod-product-compliance
Lightning Source LLC
LaVergne TN
LVHW021422110826
845150LV00007B/2036

* 9 7 8 1 4 2 5 5 0 8 7 1 5 *